THE BEST OF THE
BEST Hawai'i Local
DESSERTS

Star ★ Advertiser

Other Books by Jean Hee

ISBN-13: 978-1-56647-570-9
170 pp

ISBN-13: 978-1-56647-654-6
152 pp

ISBN-13: 978-1-56647-901-1
152 pp

ISBN-13: 978-1-56647-781-9
160 pp

ISBN-13: 978-1-56647-842-7
176 pp

ISBN-13: 978-1-56647-336-1
128 pp

ISBN-13: 978-1-56647-754-3
64 pp

ISBN-13: 978-1-56647-793-2
80 pp

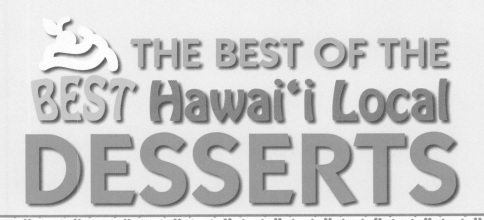

THE BEST OF THE BEST Hawai'i Local DESSERTS

Jean Watanabe Hee

with assistance from Rachel Hasegawa

photography by Kaz Tanabe

Mutual Publishing

ISBN-13: 978-1939487-77-3
Library of Congress Control Number: 2017908295

Design by Jane Gillespie
Photography by Kaz Tanabe unless otherwise noted
Illustrations from dreamstime.com; desserts ©Amornism; palm fronds ©Lanlan33

First Printing, September 2017

Mutual Publishing, LLC
1215 Center Street, Suite 210
Honolulu, Hawai'i 96816
Ph: (808) 732-1709
Fax: (808) 734-4094
e-mail: info@mutualpublishing.com
www.mutualpublishing.com

Printed in South Korea

Dedication

This cookbook is dedicated in loving memory
to my beautiful daughter, Jennifer.

Star ✦ Advertiser

Hawai'i loves its desserts. We at the *Honolulu Star-Advertiser* know this very well by reader reaction and suggestions to our coverage of Hawai'i's food every Wednesday in **Crave.**

Desserts and sweets show up everywhere in the islands—potlucks, tailgates, gatherings, and family meals, not to mention the workplace snack table or break room. Bakeries and supermarkets proudly display specialty pies, cakes, pastries, malasadas, and more. And our many fine dining restaurants pride themselves on their exquisite desserts.

Hawai'i's sweet tooth is not surprising given that many fruits—especially mango, papaya, lychee, pineapple, liliko'i, and coconut—grow in our backyard and have always been readily available.

Jean Watanabe Hee can be considered a grande dame of local cooking, authoring many best-selling recipe books. In *The Best of the Best Hawai'i Local Desserts,* Jean presents her favorite recipes in one volume.

The *Star-Advertiser* is pleased to sponsor this new volume as part of our continuing coverage of favorite island cuisine.

Enjoy.

—Dennis Francis
President and Publisher, *Honolulu Star-Advertiser*
and O'ahu Publications, Inc.

Acknowledgments

I want to thank my good friend and neighbor, Ruby Saito, for giving me the encouragement and assistance to put this cookbook together. She introduced me to new recipes that she liked and helped to test them, often improving on the original. She spent hours going through recipes with me as we decided which to keep and reject. She was a tremendous help and I truly appreciate and value her friendship.

A special thank you goes to Jeri Goodin, Ruby's granddaughter, who baked the chocolate cake and added her special touch in decorating the cake and the red velvet cupcakes, baked by Ruby, for the photo shoot for this cookbook.

I am also so very grateful to my daughter, Cheryl, who flew in from Maui to help me shop for ingredients, prep, and clean up in preparing the many desserts necessary for the photo shoot.

And finally, I want to acknowledge and thank Jane Gillespie, my graphic designer from Mutual Publishing, and Kaz Tanabe, the photographer, who with their skills, made each dessert look so special.

Contents

Introduction

Have you ever looked for a favorite dessert recipe that you remembered being in one of my cookbooks? I know that I sometimes have to think: Was it the first dessert book? Or the second?

For example, my granddaughter requested "Energy Bars with Fruits." It's light and uses dried fruits. She likes the dried cranberries in them. I finally found it in my *Best of the Best Hawai'i Recipes* on pages 156-157. It was one of the newer recipes I had included in that cookbook.

My first dessert cookbook was published in 2001, sixteen years ago. Since then there have been more wonderful recipes published in my newer cookbooks. We have our favorites from each of the cookbooks. My daughter and granddaughter requested that I consolidate and put our favorites in one cookbook. One book would make it easier and also save space.

For those who only have the first dessert book and loved it, this is your chance to discover Hawai'i's favorite dessert recipes from all my books in one new cookbook. I hope you will discover new favorites.

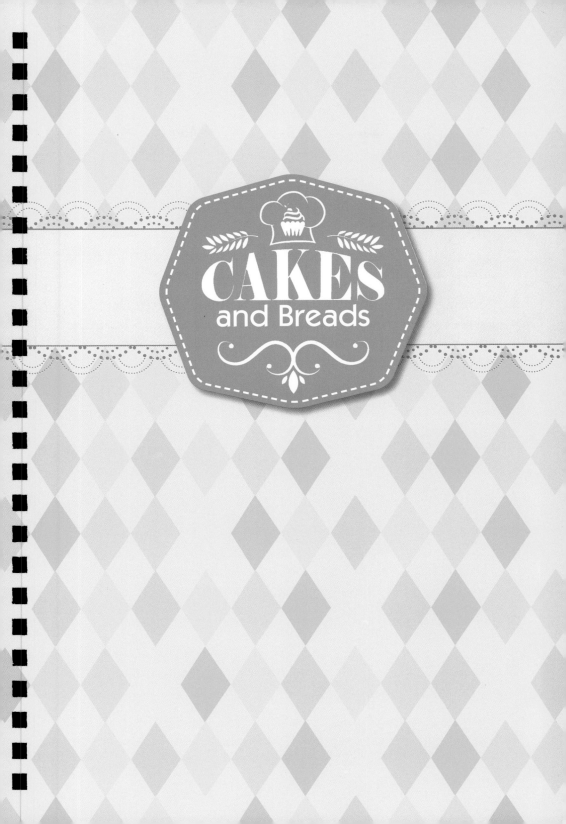

CAKES
and Breads

Cake Tips

❁ Preheat oven 10 to 15 minutes before you plan to bake.

❁ For most cakes, oven rack should be in the middle position. Some bundt and tube cakes may need to be placed on the lower rack so they don't overbrown.

❁ Allow 10 to 15 minutes for cake layers to cool before inverting onto a rack. Tube and bundt cakes need 20 minutes.

❁ Greasing and flouring: Use about 1 tablespoon shortening or butter and waxed paper or paper towel to grease a 9 x 13-inch pan. Sprinkle a tablespoon of flour into the pan, tilting pan to coat sides. Tap out excess flour.

❁ To test for doneness: ❶The cake should just be starting to pull away from the sides of the pan. ❷Press lightly with fingertips in the center of the cake. It should spring back and not indent. ❸Carefully stick a toothpick or wooden skewer in the center of the cake. It should come out clean.

❁ Sift powdered sugar to avoid lumps. Use a flour sifter or a fine-mesh strainer.

❁ Melt chocolate in a double boiler or a custard cup set in a pan of water. Do not boil the water as this will only thicken or curdle the chocolate. Water should be hot and simmering.

❁ For a child's party, fill flat-bottom ice-cream cones with cake batter half full and bake.

❁ When the oven temperature calls for 350°F lower heat to 325°F when using a glass pan to prevent overbrowning.

❁ It's better not to use a cake mix with pudding inside if you're following a recipe that calls for instant pudding as an ingredient. You could, but cake will be more wet and moist.

Apple Spice Cake

Yield: 24 servings

4 cups cored and diced apples (Fuji, Granny Smith or
  Gala)
1 cup sugar
2 cups flour
2 teaspoons baking soda
2 teaspoons cinnamon
½ teaspoon nutmeg
½ teaspoon salt
1 cup chopped walnuts or sliced almonds
2 eggs
½ cup canola oil
2 teaspoons vanilla

In large bowl, combine apples and sugar; set aside.

Sift together flour, baking soda, cinnamon, nutmeg and salt. Add to apples; mix together. Add walnuts or almonds and toss to mix well. Set aside.

Whisk together eggs, oil and vanilla until smooth. Add to apple mixture and stir until well-blended. Spread evenly in buttered 9 x 13-inch pan and bake at 350°F for 45 to 60 minutes, or until toothpick inserted in center comes out clean.

Note: Very tasty and moist! Berenice Lum who shared this recipe says she uses slightly more apples and almonds. She also uses freshly grated nutmeg and reduces it to ¼ teaspoon. Half of the amount of flour can be whole wheat flour, if desired.

Granny Smith Apple Cake

Yield: 12 servings

¾ cup chopped pecans
3 cups flour, divided
2 cups sugar, divided
2 teaspoons cinnamon
4 large Granny Smith apples, peeled, cored, and sliced
1 tablespoon baking powder
1 teaspoon salt
4 large eggs
½ cup vegetable oil
½ cup (1 block) unsalted butter, melted
¼ cup orange juice
2 teaspoons vanilla extract

Spray a 10-inch removable-bottom tube pan with nonstick spray. Sprinkle pecans evenly on bottom of pan.

In large bowl, mix 2 tablespoons of the flour, ¼ cup of the sugar, and cinnamon. Add apples and toss to combine.

In another large bowl, mix the rest of the remaining flour and 1¾ cup sugar, baking powder, and salt. Add eggs, oil, butter, orange juice and vanilla. Beat until batter is smooth. Pour half of the batter (about 2 cups) into pan. Top with half of apple mixture. Spoon remaining batter over apples and top with remaining apples, Placing them ¼-inch in from the tube and sides of pan.

Bake at 350°F for 1 hour and 20 minutes, or until toothpick inserted in the center of the cake comes out clean. Cool cake in pan on wire rack for 30 minutes. Run a paring knife around the sides and center of cake and turn cake out onto wire rack. Invert cake onto another rack to cool, apple side up.

Hint: Measure 3 cups flour first. Then take 2 tablespoons flour. Use a vegetable peeler to peel apples.

Note: Got this recipe from Karen Hamada's mom, Ellen Hamada. Jennifer and I really like this apple cake.

Apple Cake

Yield: 24 pieces

4 cups (about 3 apples) peeled and diced apples
3 eggs
1¾ cups sugar
¾ cup vegetable oil
2 cups flour
2 teaspoons cinnamon
1 teaspoon baking soda
½ teaspoon salt
1 cup chopped nuts

Grease 9 x 13-inch pan; set aside.

In large bowl, beat eggs with whisk. Add sugar and oil; mix together. Sift dry ingredients and fold into egg mixture; blend well. Add apples and nuts; mix thoroughly. Pour into greased pan and bake at 350°F for 45 minutes.

Note: Sue Sonoda, a former cafeteria manager who retired from Aliʻiōlani Elementary School, shared her tasty recipe with Ruby Saito's mother at a function at Moʻiliʻili Hongwanji Church.

Sour Cream Banana Cake

Yield: 24 servings

¾ cup butter
1½ cups sugar (or less)
2 eggs
1 teaspoon baking soda
¼ cup sour cream
1 teaspoon vanilla
½ teaspoon salt
2 cups cake flour
½ cup chopped nuts
1 cup mashed bananas

Beat butter and sugar. Add eggs and beat well. Add dry ingredients, sour cream, vanilla and nuts. Mix well. Fold in bananas. Bake in greased 9 x 9-inch pan at 325°F for 50 to 55 minutes, or until done. Check with toothpick in center of cake. It should come out clean.

Note: When I was an EPSS (Early Provisions for School Success) support teacher during the 70s, I taught at Ka'elepulu Elementary School and tasted this delicious banana cake made by a teacher there. My neighbor, Keith Shinaki, told me it was the best he ever had.

Moist Banana Cake

Yield: 24 servings

1 cup milk
1 tablespoon vinegar
1 box yellow cake mix
1 box instant vanilla pudding
1 teaspoon baking soda
2 to 3 bananas, mashed
½ cup oil
4 eggs
1 teaspoon vanilla
1 teaspoon banana extract, optional
1 cup chopped walnuts

Mix together milk and vinegar and let stand 5 minutes. Combine cake mix, instant pudding, baking soda and mashed banana. Blend together with oil, eggs, vanilla, banana extract and milk and vinegar mixture. Mix in walnuts. Pour into lightly greased 9 x 13-inch pan. Bake at 350°F for 45 minutes to 1 hour.

Note: An original recipe from my sister-in law, Evie. It is her family's favorite banana cake recipe because it is so moist. I have had so many wonderful comments from friends and strangers.

Carrot Cake

Yield: 24 servings

1½ cups flour
1⅓ cups sugar
½ cup sweetened flaked coconut
⅓ cup chopped pecans
2 teaspoons baking soda
1 teaspoon salt
2 teaspoons cinnamon
2 eggs
3 tablespoons canola oil
2 cups (about 3 large carrots) grated carrot
1 (20-ounce) can crushed pineapple, drained

In large bowl, combine flour, sugar, coconut, pecans, baking soda, salt and cinnamon; stir well with whisk. Set aside. In small bowl, beat eggs; add oil. Stir well. Add egg mixture, grated carrot and pineapple into flour mixture and mix well together. Spoon batter into 9 x 13-inch pan coated with cooking spray. Bake at 350°F for 35 minutes or until wooden toothpick in center comes out clean. Cool completely.

Frosting:
2 tablespoons butter, softened
1 (8-ounce) box cream cheese, third less fat, softened
2 to 3 cups powdered sugar, sifted (adjust to taste)
2 teaspoons vanilla
Grated carrot and pecans for garnish (optional)

In large bowl, beat butter and cream cheese at medium speed until smooth. Add powdered sugar and vanilla and beat just until smooth. Spread frosting over top of cake. Garnish each serving with grated carrot and/or pecan halves, if desired.

Note: Ruth Prinzivalli prepared this carrot cake to celebrate a birthday and all loved it. It is a lighter carrot cake with less than a third of the fat.

Butter Pound Cake

Yield: 2 (9 x 5-inch) loaf pans

1 box butter cake mix
1 (8-ounce) container sour cream
½ cup (1 block) butter, melted
¼ cup sugar
¼ cup oil
1 teaspoon vanilla
4 eggs

Mix all ingredients; pour into 2 (9 x 5-inch) greased loaf pans. Bake at 325°F for 45 minutes, or until wooden skewer inserted in middle comes out clean.

Optional: Use three medium loaf pans (8 x 3 x 2 inches) and bake for 40 minutes, or use six baby loaf pans (5 x 3 x 2 inches) and bake for 35 minutes.

Pistachio Bundt Cake

Yield: 15 servings

1 (18.25-ounce) box yellow cake mix
1 (3-ounce) box pistachio instant pudding
1 cup 7-Up® soda
1 cup oil
3 eggs
½ cup chopped nuts (optional)

Mix all ingredients, except nuts, and beat for 2 minutes on medium speed. Mix in nuts, if desired. Pour into greased and floured bundt pan. Bake at 350°F for 45 to 55 minutes.

Frosting:

1 (3-ounce) box pistachio instant pudding
2 envelopes Dream Whip®
1½ cup cold milk

Mix all ingredients and frost cooled cake.

Pistachio Nut Cake

Yield: 15 servings

1 cup chopped macadamia nuts or walnuts
½ cup sugar
2 teaspoon cinnamon
1 box yellow cake mix (e.g. Duncan Hines Classic Yel-
    low mike)
1 (3-ounce) box Jell-O® instant pistachio pudding and
    pie filling
4 eggs
⅓ cup oil
¾ cup orange juice (or water)
1 teaspoon vanilla
1 (8-ounce) container sour cream

Mix together nuts, sugar, and cinnamon. Spray bundt pan with non-stick spray and sprinkle half of nut mixture (about ⅔ cup) into bottom of bundt pan; set aside. Preheat oven to 350°F.

In large bowl, combine rest of ingredients. Beat on low speed for 1 minute to blend, then on moderate speed for about 3 minutes. Pour half of cake batter into pan. Sprinkle remaining nut mixture into pan. Pour in remaining cake batter. Bake at 45 to 50 minutes or until done. Check if pick comes out clean.

Cool in pan for 10 to 15 minutes. Run a butter knife around the cake and in the middle of pan before inverting onto a serving plate.

Note: Shared by Gwen Murai during the 2016 holidays.

Lemon Cake

Yield: 24 servings

1 (18.25-ounce) box Duncan Hines® Lemon Supreme
    cake mix
3 eggs
⅓ cup oil
1⅓ cups water
2 (3.4-ounce) boxes lemon instant pudding
1½ cups milk
Cool Whip® for topping
Lemon zest, freshly grated for sprinkling
Mint for decorating (optional)

Grease and lightly flour 9 x 13-inch pan. Preheat oven to 350°F.

In large bowl, blend cake mix, eggs, oil and water on low speed until moistened. Beat at medium speed for 2 minutes. Pour batter in prepared pan and bake immediately for 32 to 35 minutes. Cool completely when done.

Mix together lemon pudding and milk. Spread pudding over cake. Spread desired amount of Cool Whip® over. Sprinkle lemon zest over. Decorate with mint, if desired. Refrigerate for 2 hours or longer. Serve cold.

Note: At a See Dai Do picnic in 2010, James Au won 1st prize for this cake in a bake contest.

Lemon Pineapple Cake

Yield: 24 servings

1 (18.25-ounce) box Duncan Hines® Lemon Supreme
  cake mix
3 eggs
1⅓ cups water
⅓ cup vegetable oil
1 (3.4-ounce) box instant lemon pudding mix
1 (3.4-ounce) box instant vanilla pudding mix
⅔ cup milk
1 (8-ounce) container Cool Whip®
1 (20-ounce) can crushed pineapple with juice
⅓ cup finely chopped macadamia nuts
⅓ cup grated coconut (optional)

Bake cake according to package directions in greased and floured 9 x 13-inch pan.

While cake is baking, mix together pudding mixes with milk. Fold the whipped cream and instant pudding together. Refrigerate until ready to use.

When cake is done, remove cake from oven and immediately poke holes in the hot cake. Pour pineapple and juice evenly over the top. Cool cake completely.

Frost with pudding mixture. Sprinkle nuts and coconut over.

Note: People love this cake but if there are any leftover, cake will keep for a week in the refrigerator.

Lemon Apricot Cake

Yield: 20 servings

1 (18.25-ounce) box lemon cake mix
1/3 cup white sugar
3/4 cup vegetable oil
1 cup apricot nectar
4 eggs

Glaze:
2 cups powdered sugar
3 tablespoons (about 2 to 3 lemons) lemon juice
3 drops (about 1/8 teaspoon) vegetable oil

Grease 10-inch tube or bundt pan. Combine cake mix, sugar, 3/4 cup vegetable oil and apricot nectar together. Beat in eggs one at a time, mixing well after each addition. Pour batter into bundt pan. Bake at 325°F for 1 hour. Let cake cool in pan for 10 to 15 minutes.

While cake is cooling, prepare glaze. Combine powdered sugar, lemon juice and oil, mixing until smooth. Use immediately. Drizzle desired amount of glaze over warm cake creating a cobweb-type design.

Note: Very delicious and light. Icing has a light lemon flavor. Another contribution from Evelyn Shiraki.

Lemon Pound Cake

Yield: 2 loaf pans

1 (18.25-ounce) box Duncan Hines® Lemon Supreme
   cake mix
1 (8-ounce) container sour cream
½ (1 block) cup butter, melted
¼ cup oil
1 teaspoon vanilla
4 eggs

Mix all ingredients. Pour into two 9 x 5-inch greased loaf pans. Bake at 325°F for 45 minutes, or until wooden skewer inserted in middle comes out clean.

. . . .

Note: Quick and easy to make! Evie Hee used my butter pound cake recipe and substituted lemon cake mix to make a moist and lemony pound cake. She also eliminated the ¼ cup sugar the original recipe called for which made this cake less sweet!

Cream Cheese Frosting

Yield: enough for 1 dozen cupcakes

¼ cup (half block) butter, softened
1 (8-ounce) box cream cheese, softened
¾ cup (or more) powdered sugar

Beat butter and cream cheese until smooth and fluffy. Add powdered sugar and beat until well blended. Add more powdered sugar if desired.

Mandarin Peach Cake

Yield: 24 servings

1 box yellow cake mix
1 cup oil
4 eggs
1 (11-ounce) can mandarin oranges, undrained

Mix all ingredients, except mandarin oranges, and beat at medium speed until well blended. Add mandarin oranges with liquid and beat until oranges are slightly "mashed." Pour into greased 9 x 13-inch pan and bake at 350°F for 35 to 40 minutes, or until done. Cool.

Frosting:

1 (3-ounce) box instant vanilla pudding mix
1 (15-ounce) can sliced peaches, drained
1 (8-ounce) container Cool Whip®

Chop sliced peaches and place in bowl. Use electric mixer to "mash" peaches. Add vanilla pudding and beat together. Fold in Cool Whip® and blend. Frost cake.

Apple Dumpling

Yield: 24 servings

1 cup butter
1 cup sugar
2 eggs
Milk, measured in half of egg shell
3 cups flour
1 teaspoon baking powder
Salt, less than ¼ teaspoon
1 teaspoon vanilla
1 can sliced apples
1 can apple pie filling

In large bowl, beat butter and sugar; add eggs and milk. In another bowl, sift flour, baking powder and salt. Add to butter mixture; blend. Add vanilla and mix.

Spread ¾ of the dough on bottom and up the sides (halfway) of 9 x 13-inch pan. (Dough will be soft and sticky.) Spread sliced apples first and then the apple pie filling. Crisscross the rest of the dough over the filling. Bake at 375°F for 45 minutes or until brown.

Hint: The dough is very sticky and difficult to work with but the finished product is delicious. To make the crisscross lattice strips, I use a plastic sandwich bag with a little piece snipped off from one bottom corner. Place some of the sticky dough in the plastic bag and squeeze a ribbon of dough out. Start at one corner of the pan and make diagonal strips across pan. Then repeat from the opposite corner, creating a lattice look, more or less.

Note: My mom gave me this recipe 30 years ago and it still continues to be a favorite dessert. The cake-like crust at the corners are especially favored.

Bacardi® Rum Cake

Yield: 12 to 15 servings

1 box yellow cake mix
1 (3-ounce) package instant vanilla pudding
4 eggs
½ cup cold water
½ cup oil
¼ cup Bacardi® dark rum (80 proof)
1 cup chopped pecans or walnuts

In large bowl, mix all ingredients together, except nuts. Sprinkle nuts over bottom of greased and floured 10-inch tube pan or 12-cup Bundt pan. Pour batter over nuts. Bake at 325°F for 1 hour. Cool. Invert on serving plate. Glaze.

Glaze:
½ cup butter
¼ cup water
1 cup sugar
¼ cup Bacardi® dark rum

Melt butter in saucepan. Stir in water and sugar. Boil 5 minutes, stirring constantly. Remove from heat. Stir in rum. Prick top of cake. Drizzle and smooth glaze evenly over top and sides. Allow cake to absorb glaze. Repeat till glaze is used up.

Optional: Decorate with whole maraschino cherries and a border of whipped cream.

Note: If you are unsure of what dessert to bring to a potluck, this is always a sure bet to be a winner and is easy to make.

T.J.'s Sour Cream Coffee Cake

Yield: 24 servings

Dry Ingredients:
2 cups flour
1 teaspoon baking powder
1 teaspoon baking soda
½ teaspoon salt

Topping:
3 tablespoons brown sugar
½ cup chopped nuts
1 teaspoon cinnamon

Wet Ingredients:
1 cup (2 blocks) butter, softened
1 cup sugar
2 eggs
1 teaspoon vanilla
1 cup sour cream

In small bowl, mix together flour, baking powder, baking soda and salt. Set aside.

In smaller bowl, mix together topping ingredients; set aside.

In large bowl, beat butter and sugar until light and fluffy. Add eggs and beat. Add vanilla and sour cream; beat together. Add dry ingredients to butter mixture and mix together. Spread half of the batter into greased 9 x 13-inch pan. Sprinkle half of the topping mixture evenly over batter. Add remaining batter and top with remaining topping. Bake at 350°F for 30 to 35 minutes.

Note: T.J., Ruby Saito's grandson says, "Yummy, just out of the oven."

Kahlua® Cake

Yield: 24 servings

1 box yellow cake mix
1 package instant chocolate pudding
4 eggs
1 cup oil
¼ Kahlua®
¾ cup water

Mix all ingredients for 3 minutes. Pour into 9 x 13-inch pan. Bake at 350°F for 50 minutes or until done.

Topping:
½ cup powdered sugar
¼ cup Kahlua®
1 teaspoon instant coffee, powdery texture

Mix and let sit. Prick cake before pouring topping over cake.

Note: This cake tastes great even without topping. My son-in-law's mother, Ethel Hasegawa, often made this for parties and everyone loves this light cake.

Peach Bavarian

Yield: 24 servings

1 large lemon chiffon cake (vanilla or orange)
2 packages Knox® unflavored gelatin
¼ cup water
1 (29-ounce) can peaches, sliced, cut into small pieces
¾ cup sugar
1 (3-ounce) package lemon Jell-O®
2 (16-ounce) containers whipping cream
Cool Whip® (8-ounce), optional

Cut chiffon cake into 1-inch squares and fill a 9 x 13-inch pan with half of the amount. Set aside. Mix gelatin with water; set aside. Place peaches (syrup included) and sugar into saucepan and bring to a boil. Add lemon Jell-O® and the gelatin mixture and stir until dissolved. Remove and chill in refrigerator until mixture is beginning to set slightly.

In a large bowl, beat whipping cream until thick and holds peaks. Fold the chilled peach mixture into it. Pour half of the mixture all over cake pieces, working it in with a fork. Put another layer of cake pieces and then the remaining peach mixture. Top with Cool Whip®. Refrigerate.

Note: My sister-in-law, Amy, got this recipe from my Mom over 30 years ago and was. our Po-Po's favorite dessert. Everyone always asks for this recipe.

Mae's Pineapple Upside-Down Cake

Yield: 24 servings

Topping:
4 tablespoons butter
½ cup brown sugar
1 (20-ounce) can crushed pineapple in pineapple
   juice, drained
Cinnamon for sprinkling

On top of stove, using medium-low heat, melt butter in 9 x 13-inch pan. (Does not have to be completely melted.) Add brown sugar and mix together.

Add crushed pineapple and mix together quickly so it does not carmalize. Sprinkle desired amount of cinnamon and mix together. Set aside to cool. Then start making cake.

Cake:
1 cup (2 blocks) butter, softened to room temperature
2 cups sugar
4 eggs, separated into yolks and whites
3 cups cake flour
4 teaspoons baking powder
Pinch salt
1 cup milk
1 teaspoon vanilla

In large bowl, beat together butter and sugar until creamy. Add 4 egg yolks to butter mixture; beat together and set aside. In small bowl, sift together cake flour, baking powder and salt (dry ingredients); set aside. In another small bowl, combine milk and vanilla (wet ingredients).

Mix in dry and wet ingredients, alternately, to butter mixture. Whip egg whites and fold into batter. Pour over crushed pineapple in pan. Bake at 350°F for 35 to 40 minutes, or longer until done. Check for doneness. Remove from oven and cool about 15 minutes. Use butter knife to loosen sides and flip cake over onto serving platter.

Note: This is not the usual pineapple upside-down cake. Mae Ushijima of Hilo liked this version that she originally got from Mrs. Albert Kami. It's made from "scratch" and it's worth it. Very delicious!

Plum-Good Prune Cake

Yield: about 20 servings

1 (9-ounce) package pitted prunes; about 27 prunes
2 tablespoons bourbon or sherry
3 cups flour
2 teaspoons baking soda
1 teaspoon salt
1 teaspoon cinnamon
½ teaspoon cloves
1½ cups salad oil
2 cups sugar
3 eggs
2 cups (about 2 to 3 apples) coarsely shredded apples
1 cup chopped nuts
Powdered sugar, for sprinkling

Coarsely chop prunes; sprinkle with liquor, mix together and let stand several hours or overnight. Grease and flour bundt pan; set aside. Sift flour with baking soda, salt and spices. In larger bowl, beat oil with sugar and eggs for 2 minutes at medium speed. Gradually mix in dry ingredients at low speed. Mix in prunes, apples and nuts. Pour in bundt pan. Bake at 325°F for 1½ hours. Cool in pan for 15 minutes. Invert onto cooling rack to cool completely. Sprinkle with powdered sugar.

Note: Highly recommended by Kathryn Kato as one of her family favorites. Don't let the word "prune" scare you. Try it. You might like it.

Chiffon Cake

Yield: 15 servings

2 cups flour, sifted
1½ cups sugar
3 teaspoons baking powder
1 teaspoon salt
½ cup oil
6 large egg yolks, unbeaten
¾ cup cold water
2 teaspoons almond extract
½ teaspoon cream of tartar
1 cup egg whites (from 8 large eggs)

Sift first four ingredients together. Make a well and add oil, egg yolks, water and almond extract. Beat until smooth. (With electric mixer, use medium speed for 1 minute.) In large bowl, add cream of tartar to egg whites; beat at high speed for 3 to 5 minutes until whites form very stiff peaks. Do not underbeat. Preheat oven 325°F.

Pour egg yolk mixture gradually over beaten egg whites, gently folding with rubber scraper just until blended. Do not stir. Pour immediately into ungreased 10-inch tube pan. Bake at 325°F for 55 minutes, then increase to 350°F for 10 to 15 minutes, or until top springs back when lightly touched. Turn pan upside down, placing tube over neck of funnel or bottle. Let hang until cold. Loosen with spatula. Turn pan over, hit edge sharply on table to loosen.

Note: A very light cake. This recipe was passed down from Aunty Clara (Chun) and is so often requested that Diane Au always makes it for family gatherings.

Avocado Cake

Yield: three 8-inch cake pans

¾ cup shortening
2 cups sugar
3 eggs
2²/₃ cups sifted flour
¾ teaspoon cinnamon
¾ teaspoon allspice
¾ teaspoon salt
1¼ teaspoons baking soda
¾ cup sour milk*
1½ cups ripe avocado, mashed
½ cup chopped dates
¾ cup chopped macadamia nuts
¾ cup raisins
¼ cup sugar mixed with 1 teaspoon cinnamon for
    sprinkling

In large bowl, beat together shortening and sugar until fluffy; add eggs one at a time, beating after each egg. In medium bowl, sift together flour, cinnamon, allspice and salt.

Dissolve baking soda in sour milk. Into large bowl of beaten shortening mixture, mix in avocado, sifted flour and spices, adding alternately with sour milk; mix well. Fold dates, nuts and raisins into batter. Pour batter into 3 greased and floured 8 x 8-inch pans. Sprinkle desired amount of sugar/cinnamon over. Bake at 350°F for 35 to 40 minutes. Check for doneness with toothpick.

*To make sour milk, mix in 1 teaspoon vinegar or lemon juice to 1 cup whole or 2 percent milk. Let sit for 10 to 15 minutes. The milk should begin to curdle slightly. So for ¾ cup sour milk, I added about ¾ teaspoon vinegar to ¾ cup milk.

Note: Thanks to my good friend, Ruby Saito, who is always on the lookout for avocado recipes. She got this recipe from a friend via Maui.

Liliko'i Bundt Cake

Yield: 10 to 12 servings

1 cup (2 blocks) unsalted butter, softened
2 cups sugar, divided
4 eggs
3 cups flour
1½ teaspoons baking powder
½ teaspoon baking soda
1 teaspoon salt
1 cup Greek yogurt
1 cup liliko'i juice

Spray 10-inch bundt pan with nonstick spray; set aside.

In large bowl, beat butter and 1½ cups of the sugar for 2 minutes. Beat in eggs, one at a time until blended. Then beat 2 to 3 minutes more until very fluffy.

In another bowl, sift together flour, baking powder, baking soda, and salt; set aside.

In small bowl, whisk yogurt, remaining ½ cup of sugar, and Iilliko'i juice until well-blended.

Add ⅓ of flour mixture to butter mixture and mix just until blended. Pour in half of yogurt mixture; mix again. Add rest of flour and yogurt mixture in the same way, ending with folding in final flour mixture. Do not over mix. Pour batter into prepared pan. Bake at 350°F for 40 to 50 minutes or until toothpick inserted into cake comes our mostly clean.

Amy's Sponge Cake

Yield: 12 servings

Orange zest from 2 oranges (about 2 to 3 teaspoons)
½ cup (about 2 oranges) fresh orange juice
10 eggs, separated
1½ teaspoons cream of tartar
1 cup sugar, divided use
1 cup cake flour
2½ teaspoons baking powder
½ teaspoon salt
½ cup vegetable oil
1 teaspoon vanilla

Finely grate orange skin for orange zest; set aside. Squeeze oranges for juice; set aside.

In medium bowl, beat egg whites, cream of tartar and ½ cup of the sugar on high speed for 7 minutes; set aside.

In large bowl, sift cake flour, remaining ½ cup of sugar, baking powder and salt. Add oil, egg yolks, vanilla, orange juice and orange zest and beat on medium speed for 15 minutes. Fold in egg white; pour into ungreased tube pan. Bake at 325°F for 35 to 40 minutes or until top is brown. (Do not open oven door while baking.) Check for doneness with pick or skewer. Invert over bottle and cool over 2 hours. Slide knife around sides and center to release cake.

Note: This is my favorite cake made by my sister-in-law, Amy Hee. It is silky smooth and moist. Amy said the large 10 fl. oz. Worcestershire Sauce bottle is a perfect size to place the inverted tube pan. She also recommended that the cake cool away from wind.

Pumpkin Crunch

Yield: 9 x 13-inch pan

1 (29-ounce) can solid-pack pumpkin
1 (13-ounce) can evaporated milk
1 cup sugar
3 eggs, slightly beaten
¼ teaspoon cinnamon
1 box yellow pudding cake mix
1 cup chopped walnuts
1 cup butter, melted

Mix pumpkin, evaporated milk, sugar, eggs and cinnamon together. Pour into 9 x 13-inch pan lined with waxed paper. Pour 1 box cake mix (dry) over pumpkin mixture and pat nuts on cake mix. Spoon melted butter evenly over nuts. Bake at 350°F for 50 to 60 minutes. Invert onto tray and peel off waxed paper. When slightly cooled, spread frosting over.

Frosting:

1 (8-ounce) package cream cheese, room temperature
½ cup powdered sugar, sifted
¾ cup Cool Whip®

Beat together cream cheese and powdered sugar. Fold in Cool Whip®. Spread over cake evenly. Refrigerate. Cut into squares.

Note: My son-in-law's favorite at Thanksgiving, but a great dessert any time of the year.

Dobash Cake

Yield: 24 servings

1 (18.25-ounce) box devil's food cake mix
3 eggs
½ cup oil
1 can 7-Up®

Mix all ingredients and bake in greased 9 x 13-inch pan at 350°F for 35 to 40 minutes. Cool before frosting.

Frosting:
1 cup water
1 cup sugar
¼ cup (½ stick) butter
¼ teaspoon salt
⅓ cup cornstarch
½ cup Nestlé's® Nesquick Chocolate Flavor
½ cup water

Boil together 1½ cup water, sugar, butter and salt. Combine cornstarch, Nesquick® and ½ cup water; add to boiling mixture. Cook until it thickens, stirring constantly. Cool completely before frosting cake. Refrigerate any leftover cake.

. . . .

Note: Delicious! Easy to make. Cake is light and moist. After refrigeration, cake still tastes great the next day.

Chocolate Cake

Yield: 16 servings

2 cups flour
2 cups sugar
¾ cup unsweetened cocoa
1 teaspoon salt
1 teaspoon baking powder
2 teaspoons baking soda
1 cup vegetable oil
1 cup hot coffee
1 cup milk
2 eggs, slightly beaten
1 teaspoon vanilla

Preheat oven 325°F. Grease and flour two round 9-inch cake pans.

Sift together dry ingredients. Add oil, coffee and milk; beat at medium speed for 2 minutes. Add eggs and vanilla; beat 2 more minutes. Pour into cake pans. Bake for 25 to 30 minutes or until toothpick inserted in center comes out clean. Cool on wire racks for 15 minutes. Turn cakes out on rack and cool completely.

Frosting:
1 cup milk
5 tablespoons flour
½ cup (1 block) butter, softened
½ cup Crisco®
1 cup sugar
1 teaspoon vanilla

Combine milk and flour in saucepan; cook on medium low, stirring constantly, about 10 minutes, until thick. Cover and refrigerate.

In medium mixing bowl, beat together butter and Crisco®. Add sugar and vanilla; beat until creamy. Add chilled milk and flour mixture; beat for 5 to 10 minutes.

If necessary, use a serrated knife to trim off any domed part from tops of cake. To frost cake, carefully separate cake from wire rack and place one cake layer, top side down, on a serving plate. Frost evenly on top of cake layer. Place the other layer, top side down, on the first layer. Spread frosting over top and sides.

. . . .

Note: Great tasting cake! Very moist. I found that Williams-Sonoma Gold Touch® nonstick round cake pans are best for easy baking. Do grease and flour, however. The cakes come out even on top and turn out easily.

Chocolate Cherry Cake

Yield: 24 servings

4 eggs
1 cup oil
1 (16.5-ounce) box Duncan Hines® Devil's Food cake mix
1 (21-ounce) can cherry pie filling

In large bowl, beat eggs. Add oil; beat together. Add cake mix; mix well. Fold cherry pie filling into batter. Pour into greased 9 x 13-inch pan. Bake at 325°F for approximately 40 minutes or until done. Test for doneness with toothpick inserted in middle.

. . . .

Note: Very moist and delicious! Another recipe shared by Pearl N. Takahashi. You must try this! Everyone loves this and it uses only four ingredients.

The Ultimate Chocolate Cake

1 (18.5-ounce) box chocolate cake mix with pudding
in mix
½ cup cocoa
3 eggs
1 cup mayonnaise
1⅓ cups water

In large bowl, beat together cake mix and cocoa. Add remaining ingredients; beat until just blended. Beat at medium speed 2 minutes. Pour into greased and floured 9 x 13-inch pan. Bake at 350°F for 30 to 35 minutes or until toothpick inserted in center comes out clean.

Chocolate Frosting:
6 tablespoons margarine, room temperature
¾ cup cocoa
3½ cups powdered sugar
6 to 7 tablespoons milk
1 teaspoon vanilla

In small bowl, beat margarine. Combine cocoa and sugar and add to margarine, beating alternately with milk. Beat until of spreading consistency, adding an additional 1 tablespoon of milk, if needed. Add vanilla. Makes 2¾ cups.

Cocoa Cake

2½ cups flour
1½ cups sugar
½ cup cocoa
2 teaspoons baking soda, sifted
½ teaspoon salt
²⁄₃ cup oil
2 tablespoons white vinegar
1 tablespoon vanilla
2 cups cold coffee or cold water

Topping:
¼ cup sugar
½ teaspoon cinnamon

Mix first 5 ingredients. Stir with fork to mix. Add next 4 ingredients and stir with fork until well mixed. DO NOT BEAT. Pour into ungreased 9 x 13-inch pan. Combine sugar and cinnamon; sprinkle over batter. Bake at 350°F for 30 to 35 minutes.

Note: This chocolate cake is so moist that it doesn't need frosting. Linda Kealoha, a teacher, has shared this recipe many times at school potlucks because it is such a favorite with the faculty.

Chocolate Surprise

Yield: 30 servings

1 (8-ounce) box cream cheese, softened
½ cup sugar
1 egg
1 (18.25-ounce) box Duncan Hines® Devil's Food cake mix
1 (3-ounce) box instant vanilla pudding
3 eggs
½ cup oil
1 cup water
1 cup chocolate chips, or use less (optional)

Beat cream cheese and sugar together. Add 1 egg and beat well. Set aside. Mix together cake mix, instant vanilla pudding, 3 eggs, oil and water at low speed until moistened. Then beat at medium speed until well blended (about 2 minutes).

Pour half of cake batter into greased 9 x 13-inch pan. Cover with cream cheese batter. Carefully spread rest of chocolate batter over. Sprinkle desired amount of chocolate chips over. Bake at 325°F for 45 to 50 minutes or until done.

Note: Winifred Hee shared this recipe that she got from a friend. She said it was good. After I made it, I agree. It is good! And my neighbors also agree. It tastes great with or without the chocolate chips.

Cherry Chocolate Cake

Yield: 24 servings

1 (15.25-ounce) box devil's food cake mix
1 cup water
⅓ cup vegetable oil
3 eggs
1 (3-ounce) package cherry Jell-O®
1 cup hot water

Bake chocolate cake mix as directed on label. Dissolve cherry Jell-O® in hot water. Cool. When cake is done, poke holes into cake with chopstick. Pour cooled Jell-O® into holes and over cake.

Topping:

1 (3.9-ounce) box instant chocolate pudding
1 cup cold milk
1 (8-ounce) container Cool Whip®
1 can Comstock® cherry pie filling

Beat chocolate pudding and milk. Fold in Cool Whip®. Frost cake. Carefully, spoon cherry pie filling over top, spreading cherries evenly. Refrigerate to set before serving.

Note: Very pretty and festive looking. It's light and not too sweet, and it tastes even better the next day. Many have commented that they like this cake very much even though they usually don't care for cakes.

Triple Chocolate Cake

Yield: 24 to 30 servings

1 (15.25-ounce) box devil's food cake mix
1 (3-ounce) box instant chocolate pudding mix
½ cup water
½ cup oil
4 eggs
1 (8-ounce) container sour cream
3 to 4 teaspoons instant coffee
1 (12-ounce) bag mini chocolate morsels or less

Beat all ingredients together (except chocolate chips) with mixer until smooth. Stir in chocolate chips. Pour into greased 9 x 13-inch pan. Bake at 350°F for 45 minutes. Cool completely. Sprinkle with powdered sugar, if desired, or frost with your favorite frosting.

Note: At a potluck luncheon at Mutsumi Pang's home we were served this triple chocolate cake, one of many desserts offered that day. Mutsumi had baked this very easy and tasty cake which we enjoyed. She said she found this recipe in a Hilo cookbook put together many years ago by the Church of the Holy Cross. She added her little touch by mixing in instant coffee.

Sour Cream Chocolate Cake

1 (15.25-ounce) box chocolate cake mix or devil's food
    chocolate cake mix
1 (3-ounce) box instant vanilla pudding or chocolate
    pudding mix
4 eggs
¾ cup salad oil
⅓ cup Kahlua®, optional
2 cups sour cream
½ cup chocolate chips

Combine cake mix and instant pudding. In a separate bowl, beat eggs and add oil, Kahlua® and sour cream. Beat well. Add to cake mixture and mix thoroughly. Mix in chocolate chips. Pour into greased and floured bundt pan (or lightly greased 9 x 13-inch pan). Bake at 350°F for 45 to 60 minutes.

Holiday Spice Cake

Yield: 3 medium loaf pans (8 x 3 x 2-inches)

4 cups flour
1 teaspoon salt
½ teaspoon cinnamon
½ teaspoon nutmeg
1 cup (2 blocks) butter, softened
2 cups light brown sugar, packed
1 cup white sugar
4 large eggs
1 cup sour cream
1 teaspoon baking soda
2 tablespoons brandy (or whiskey)
2 cups coarsely chopped walnuts
1½ cups golden raisins
2 cups diced mixed candied fruits (or cranberries)

Spray nonstick spray into three 5 x 3 x 2-inch loaf pans, then line pans with baking parchment paper and spray nonstick spray on paper. Set aside.

Sift together flour, salt, cinnamon, and nutmeg; set aside.

In large bowl, beat butter and sugars until fluffy. Add eggs, one at a time, beating well after each addition. Blend in sour cream. Dissolve baking soda in brandy and add to mixture.

Gradually beat in flour mixture until smooth. Fold in nuts, raisins, and candied fruits. Place into pans. Bake at 275°F for 1 hour and 45 minutes or until pick inserted into center comes out clean. Let stand 20 minutes then remove to wire rack to cool completely.

Note: Got this recipe from my good friend, Ruby Saito, and made it for my church friends. They loved it!

Coconut Cake

Yield: 24 servings

1 (18.5-ounce) box yellow cake mix
1 (3.4-ounce) box instant vanilla pudding
½ cup vegetable oil
4 eggs
½ teaspoon vanilla
1 (13.5-ounce) can coconut milk

Glaze:
2 cups powdered sugar, sifted
⅓ cup water
1 teaspoon vanilla
2 tablespoons butter, melted

Preheat oven 350°F. Grease 9 x 13-inch pan.

Beat together all cake ingredients (except coconut milk). When combined, mix in coconut milk. Pour into greased pan and bake for 35 to 40 minutes.

While cake is baking, mix together glaze ingredients until well blended. When cake is done, poke holes in hot cake with a fork. Spoon glaze evenly over.

Note: Recipe was given to Evelyn Shiraki from her friend and shared with others. The cake is easy to prepare and tasty.

Coconut-Pineapple Cream Cake

Yield: 20 servings

Cake:
1 box Duncan Hines® Lemon Supreme cake mix
4 eggs
½ cup oil
1 cup 7-Up®

Combine all ingredients and beat 3 minutes. Bake in a well-greased and floured 9 x 13-inch pan at 350°F for 30 to 35 minutes. Cool.

Cream Cheese Topping:
1 (8-ounce) package cream cheese
1 (12-ounce) can frozen coconut milk, thawed
1 (3-ounce) box instant vanilla pudding

Whip together all ingredients and spread over cooled cake.

Pineapple Coconut Topping:
1 (16-ounce) can crushed pineapple, drained
1 (8-ounce) container Cool Whip®
1 can fresh frozen coconut or 1⅓ cups shredded coconut

Spread pineapple over cream-cheese topping. Then spread Cool Whip® over pineapple. Sprinkle coconut. Refrigerate.

Cream Puff Cake

Yield: 24 servings

Crust:
1 cup water
½ cup (1 block) butter or margarine
1 cup flour
4 eggs

Boil water and margarine on medium heat. Add flour all at once. Quickly stir with wooden spoon until mixture comes off the sides of the pot. Place in large mixing bowl. Cool about 10 minutes. Add eggs, one at a time, beating well after each one. Spread into greased 9 x 13-inch pan. Bake at 400°F for 30 minutes. Set aside to cool.

Filling:
1 (8-ounce) box cream cheese , softened to room
    temperature
2 (3.9-ounce) boxes instant pudding, flavor of your
    choice
2½ cups milk

Topping:
1 (8-ounce) container Cool Whip®
Chocolate syrup for drizzling (optional)

Beat cream cheese until fluffy. Add pudding and milk. Continue to beat at low moderate speed until smooth, scraping sides with spatula to help smooth out lumps. Spread mixture onto cooled crust. Spread Cool Whip® over and drizzle chocolate syrup, if desired.

Note: Thank you, Keith Won. This is a big favorite of my family. They think it's the greatest! Keith said the recipe originally came from Kandyce who made it with chocolate pudding with caramel chips. I made it with chocolate pudding since I had that in my cupboard and everyone loved it!

New York Style Cheesecake

Yield: 12 servings

15 (30 squares) graham crackers, crushed
3 to 4 tablespoons butter, melted

Filling:
4 (8-ounce) boxes cream cheese, softened
1½ cups sugar
¾ cup milk
4 eggs
1 cup sour cream
1 tablespoon vanilla
¼ cup flour

Crust:

In medium bowl, mix together crushed graham crackers with melted butter. Press onto bottom of greased 9-inch springform pan. Set aside.

Filling:

In large bowl, beat cream cheese with sugar until smooth. Blend in milk and mix in eggs one at a time, mixing just enough to incorporate. Mix in sour cream, vanilla and flour until smooth. Pour into prepared crust. Bake in preheated 350°F oven for 1 hour. Turn oven off and let cake cool in oven with door closed for 5 to 6 hours. (Prevents cake from cracking.) Refrigerate until serving.

Note: Dr. Clayton Chong, my oncologist, is such a great cook! He was on a search for a cheesecake like the one he enjoyed in New York. After trying out many recipes, (he said one was so terrible he just dumped it) he found this to be the best so far. He's made this many times sharing with his family and friends. They all love it.

Sour Cream Cake

Yield: 24 servings

1 (16.5-ounce) box Duncan Hines® Classic Yellow cake
   mix or use any flavor
½ cup (1 block) butter, melted and cooled
1 cup sour cream
4 eggs
½ cup oil
1 teaspoon vanilla

Lightly grease 9 x 13-inch pan.

Place all ingredients in large bowl. Beat at low speed until moistened (about 30 seconds). Beat at medium speed for 2 minutes. Pour into pan and bake at 325°F for 45 to 60 minutes. Cake is done when toothpick inserted in center comes out clean. Cool on wire rack at least 15 minutes before frosting. Frost with Easy Frosting below.

Easy Frosting

Yield: ¾ cup

½ cup whipping cream
1 cup semi-sweet chocolate chips
1 teaspoon vanilla

Heat whipping cream until just ready to boil. BUT DO NOT BOIL. Remove from heat; add chocolate chips and stir until chips are melted. Add vanilla. Pour over cooled cake.

Note: Cake is similar to a pound cake. It does need the frosting to add to the flavor. Refrigerate any left over cake. In fact, I liked it cold the next day.

Suggestion: Use as hot fudge sauce or as a dip for strawberries.

Creamsicle Cake

1 box white cake mix with pudding
1 (3-ounce) box orange Jell-O®
1 cup boiling water
½ cup cold water

Bake cake according to directions on box. Cool. Dissolve Jell-O® in boiling water and add cold water. Cool. Use large end of chopstick to poke holes in cake. Use spoon to pour Jell-O® over cake and into holes.

Frosting:
1 (3-ounce) box instant vanilla pudding
1 cup milk
1 (8-ounce) container Cool Whip®
1 teaspoon vanilla
1 teaspoon orange extract

Beat vanilla pudding and milk until thickened. Mix in Cool Whip®, vanilla and orange extract until well blended. Frost cake and refrigerate.

Note: Fantastic! Tastes like an ice cream cake and is super easy to prepare.

Perfect Vanilla Cupcakes

Yield: 1 dozen cupcakes

¾ cup (1½ blocks) butter, softened
1 cup sugar
1½ cups flour
1½ teaspoons baking powder
½ teaspoon salt
3 eggs
1 tablespoon warm water
1 teaspoon vanilla extract

Beat butter and sugar until light and fluffy. In smaller bowl, combine flour, baking powder and salt; whisk together. Starting and ending with an egg, alternate adding eggs and flour to butter mixture, beating until well blended together. Beat in water and vanilla until just mixed. Pour into cupcake paper lined muffin pan. Bake at 400°F for 15 to 17 minutes or until cooked and golden. Remove from oven and let stand for a few minutes before turning them onto a wire rack to cool.

Note: Oven rack should be in the lower middle position. When cupcakes cool frost with your favorite frosting. See page 15 for Cream Cheese Frosting or page 48 for Chocolate Frosting recipes.

Note: Highly recommended by my daughter, Jennifer, who loves cupcakes.

Siren Chocolate Cupcakes

Yield: 32 to 35 cupcakes

4 (4-ounce) squares unsweetened chocolate, (e.g.
   Baker's® unsweetened baking chocolate squares)
½ cup (1 block) butter
2 eggs
2 cups buttermilk
2 teaspoons vanilla
2 ½ cups sifted cake flour
2 cups sugar
2 teaspoons baking soda

Melt butter and chocolate in saucepan on low heat.

In medium bowl, beat eggs until thick (about 2 minutes). Add buttermilk and vanilla; beat and set aside.

Sift cake flour, sugar and baking soda 3 times into large bowl. Pour egg mixture into dry ingredients and stir with spoon. Add melted butter and chocolate; stir with spoon until mixed well. Then beat with electric mixer 1 to 2 minutes. Pour into paper-lined cupcake pans, about ¾ full. Bake at 350°F for 15 minutes, or until done. When cool, frost with Chocolate Frosting. (See page 48)

. . . .

Note: Catherine Thomas is often asked to make this delicious chocolate cake for family gatherings. "It is so easy," she says. She recommends using real vanilla extract, Darigold butter, Meadow gold buttermilk and Island eggs for best results. Do not overbeat chocolate and butter or it will get lumpy. "You want a smooth texture."

Variation: Pour batter into 9 x 13-inch pan which has been greased, lined with waxed paper and greased lightly again. Or grease and flour pan. Bake at 350°F for 40 minutes, or until done.

Red Velvet Cupcakes

Yield: 24 to 30 cupcakes

1 (16.5-ounce) box Duncan Hines Red Velvet cake mix
1 (3.4-ounce) box vanilla instant pudding
1 cup sour cream
½ cup water
½ cup vegetable oil
3 eggs
1 cup miniature semi-sweet chocolate chips (optional)

Preheat oven 350°F. Line cupcake cups with cupcake liners.

In large bowl combine cake mix, instant pudding, sour cream, water, oil, and eggs. Blend on low for 30 seconds. Then beat on medium speed for 2 minutes, occasionally scraping sides of bowl. (Mixture will be thick.) Spoon batter into each cupcake liner about ½ to ¾ full. Bake for 20 to 22 minutes or until done. Test with toothpick in center of cupcake. Cool thoroughly before frosting.*

Note: Ruby Saito tweaked the original recipe from Linda Shimamoto and made it much simpler to bake. The recipe makes 24 very high cupcakes but Ruby preferred 30 cupcakes and a little mound of frosting on top. So pretty and petite and so delicious.

*See suggested Cream Cheese Frosting on page 15.

Miniature Cream Cheesecake

Yield: 30 little mini cakes

2 (8-ounce) packages cream cheese, softened
¾ cup sugar
1 teaspoon vanilla
2 eggs
1 (21-ounce) can cherry or blueberry pie filling
1 (11-ounce) box vanilla wafers

Combine cream cheese, sugar, vanilla and eggs. Beat with electric mixer until blended. Place 1 wafer, flat side down, in each 2-inch mini foil baking cup. (Discard paper separators.) Fill with about 1 tablespoonful of mixture. Place baking cups directly on cookie sheet. Bake at 350°F for 15 minutes. Cool. Top with pie filling. Refrigerate.

Chocolate Frosting

Yield: about 2½ cups

1 (16-ounce) box powdered sugar
½ cup evaporated milk
2 teaspoons vanilla
½ cup (1 block) butter
4 (4-ounce) squares unsweetened chocolate

Sift powdered sugar into medium bowl. Add evaporated milk and vanilla; mix together. Set aside.

Melt butter and chocolate square over low heat and add to powdered sugar mixture. Beat well. Frost cooled cake.

. . . .

Note: Catherine Thomas uses this frosting for her Siren Chocolate Cupcakes. (See page 46.) Need not be refrigerated.

Jeri's Easy Trifle

Yield: 15 to 20 servings

1 (16.5-ounce) box chocolate cake mix, bake according to box directions
2 (3.9-ounce) boxes instant chocolate pudding, prepare according to box directions
1 to 2 (8-ounce) containers Cool Whip®
Oreo® cookies, crushed

Optional Toppings:
Nuts, chocolate chips, M&M's®, chopped up candies
   (e.g. Andes® Mint candy gives a nice flavor)

Follow cake box directions and bake cake in 9 x 13-inch pan. Cool.

Prepare chocolate pudding as directed. Chill.

Cut cake into ½-inch cubes and place half of the amount in large bowl.* Pat down into bottom of bowl and cover with half of the pudding. Cover with half amount of Cool Whip®. Sprinkle with crushed Oreo® cookies. Repeat layer and add optional toppings. Refrigerate at least 1 hour or until ready to serve.

*Use one large bowl or divide into smaller bowls.

Variation: Jeri Goodin likes to experiment with different combinations. For a patriotic fruit variation, use red velvet cake mix, vanilla pudding, Cool Whip® sliced strawberries, blueberries and white chocolate chips.

Optional: Use few drops of blue color to Cool Whip®.

Interesting Footnote: Jeri Goodin was a kindergarten student in my classroom at 'Aikahi Elenebtary School many years ago. She graduated from Le Jardin Academy and is a recent graduate of University of Find-lay in Ohio. She and her mother, Kelly, and grandmother, Ruby Saito, all love to bake and create.

Fruit Cake

Yield: 3 small loaf pans

1 (8-ounce) box cream cheese, room temperature
1 cup (2 blocks) butter, room temperature
1½ cups sugar
1½ teaspoons vanilla
4 eggs, room temperature
2½ cups flour
1½ teaspoons baking powder
½ cup chopped nuts
1 cup mixed candied fruits (or dried cranberry, blue-
    berry, etc.)

Spray 3 loaf pans (8 x 3 x 2-inches) with nonstick cooking spray; set aside.

Beat together cream cheese, butter and sugar well. Add vanilla and eggs; beat together. Add flour and baking powder; mix thoroughly with a heavy spoon. Stir in nuts and fruit.

Spoon batter into pans. Bake at 325°F for 55 minutes.

Note: A very light fruit cake which I really liked. This is not the tradi-tional type but one that is easier to make and enjoy. More like a pound cake with fruit cake mixed in to celebrate the holidays.

Breakfast Bread Pudding

Yield: 24 servings

1 cup sugar
2 cups milk
½ cup (1 block) butter
1 teaspoon vanilla
6 eggs, whisked well
12 mini croissants (stale is better)
1 (8-ounce) box cream cheese
1 (21-ounce) can apple pie filling
Cinnamon for sprinkling

In sauce pan, combine sugar, milk and butter. Heat on medium-low and bring to slight boil, stirring occasionally. Remove from heat; cool. Add vanilla and well-whisked eggs; mix thoroughly.

Spray 9 x 13-inch pan with non-stick spray. Cut croissants in half lengthwise and line pan with half the amount. Slice cream cheese in thin slices and line over croissants. Layer remaining croissants over. Pour milk mixture over croissants. Spread apple pie filling over. Sprinkle cinnamon over all. Bake at 350°F for 30 minutes. Serve either hot or cold.

Note: It's called a breakfast pudding but I also consider it a fantastic pastry dessert. Gwen Murai sent me this great recipe. Gwen got it from Pearl N. Takahashi who got it from Elsie Higa Miike. We're all classmates from Hilo High class of 1957. I am so thankful for all the sharing of recipes.

Note: If you're out of milk, Pearl used one can evaporated milk and added enough water to total 2 cups.

Suggestion: Our Popo preferred peaches to apples so I have also used peach pie filling in place of the apple pie filling and eliminated the cinnamon. You can also substitute with blueberry pie filling, if desired.

Quick 'n Easy Bread Pudding

Yield: 24 to 30 pieces

½ cup (1 stick) butter
1¼ cups sugar
4 eggs
1 teaspoon vanilla
½ cup raisins
1 pound day old bread, cubed
6 cups milk
Cinnamon, for sprinkling

Beat butter and sugar thoroughly. Add eggs and vanilla; beat well. Add raisins to mixture; mix together. Set aside.

Mix bread and milk together. Add to first mixture; mix thoroughly. Pour into greased 9 x 13-inch pan. Sprinkle top with cinnamon. Bake at 350°F for 1 hour. Cut after cooling.

Fuji Apple Bread Pudding

Yield: 24 servings

9 eggs
1¾ cups sugar
1 teaspoon cinnamon
1 teaspoon vanilla
½ teaspoon salt
2 (12-ounce) cans evaporated milk
3 cups water
½ cup (1 block) butter
1 King's Hawaiian® sweet bread, cubed
½ to 1 cup raisins
2 Fuji apples

In medium bowl, beat eggs with whisk. Add sugar, cinnamon, vanilla and salt; mix thoroughly. Set aside.

Heat evaporated milk, water and butter until butter melts. Remove from heat; cool slightly. Combine egg mixture into milk mixture.

Cut apples into fourths. Core, peel and slice thinly. In large bowl, combine bread, raisins and apples. Pour milk mixture over. Gently mix together and let soak in refrigerator at least 30 minutes. Pour into greased 9 x 13-inch pan and bake at 325°F for 1 hour and 5 minutes.

Note: Refrigerate any leftover bread pudding. It tastes even better the next day, especially with a hot cup of coffee.

King's Hawaiian®
Sweet Bread-Bread Pudding

Yield: 9 x 13-inch pan

1 (16-ounce) King's Hawaiian® Sweet Bread
Raisins, cinnamon, nutmeg for sprinkling
3 cups milk
1 cup sugar
1½ cups butter, melted
9 eggs, beaten
1½ teaspoons vanilla

Break bread into large pieces. Place into buttered 9 x 13-inch pan. Sprinkle raisins, cinnamon and nutmeg over bread pieces. In saucepan, combine milk, sugar and butter; heat to boiling point. Remove from heat; add beaten eggs. (Be careful that milk mixture is not so hot that it could curdle eggs.) Add vanilla; mix and pour over bread, making sure bread is soaked. Sprinkle more cinnamon and nutmeg over pudding, if desired. Bake at 350°F for 20 to 25 minutes or until knife inserted in middle of pudding comes out clean.

Pineapple Banana Bread

Yield: 6 baby loaf pans

4 eggs
1 cup vegetable oil
2½ cups flour
1½ cups sugar
2 teaspoons baking powder
2 teaspoons baking soda
1 teaspoons salt
2 cups (about 4 to 5 bananas) mashed bananas
1 (8-ounce) can crushed pineapple , drained
½ cup nuts (optional)

Grease 6 baby loaf pans (5¾ x 3¼ x 2-inches).*

In large bowl, whisk eggs and add oil. Sift dry ingredients together and mix into egg mixture; blend well. Mix together mashed bananas and crushed pineapple. Add to mixture. Add nuts, if desired. Ladle equal amounts into pans. Bake at 350°F for 40 to 45 minutes. Check with toothpick inserted in center for doneness.

Note: At one of our '57 Hilo High class luncheons, Doris Tanaka Ni-iyama made this and I really liked the taste. She said she was using my "Chocolate Banana Bread" recipe from *Hawai'i's Best Local Desserts* and discovered that she didn't have enough mashed bananas. So, being the creative person she is, she used crushed pineapple to make up the difference.

*You may also use two 9 x 5-inch loaf pans. Bake at 350°F for 1 hour. Or three 8 x 3¾ x 2½-inch loaf pans. Bake at 350°F for 45 minutes. Doris used her small bundt pan.

T.D.'s Banana Bread

Yield: 3 medium loaf pans (8 x 3 x 2-inches)

1 cup (2 blocks) butter, softened
2 cups sugar
4 eggs, beaten well
2½ cups flour
1 teaspoon salt
2 teaspoons baking soda
7 ripe bananas (about 3 cups)
½ cup walnuts, chopped (optional)

Grease 3 medium loaf pans or use nonstick spray; set aside.

In large bowl, beat butter and sugar until fluffy. Add beaten eggs; mix together. Sift dry ingredients and add to mixture; blend well. Mix in mashed banana. Add nuts, if desired. Pour into loaf pans. Bake at 350°F for 50 to 55 minutes or until done. Test for doneness.

Hint: With nuts, bake for 55 minutes. Without nuts, for 50 minutes.

Note: At one of our class luncheons, Takako Desaki shared her delicious banana bread and willingly shared her recipe with us.

Mango Bread

Yield: 2 medium loaf pans (8 x 3 x 2-inches)

2 cups flour
1½ cups sugar
2 teaspoons baking soda
1 teaspoon cinnamon
2 cups diced mangoes
3 eggs, beaten
1 cup vegetable oil
½ cup chopped nuts

Grease 2 medium loaf pans; set aside.

In large bowl, sift together flour, sugar, baking soda, and cinnamon. Add mangoes, eggs, and oil; blend together. Mix in nuts. Pour evenly into greased pans. Bake at 350°F for 50 to 55 minutes or until done. Test with toothpick.

Note: Berenice Lum freezes her extra mangoes when there is an abundance during mango season and bakes loaves of mango bread for the bake sale at St. Ann's Christmas Festival. They sell out quickly!

Corn Bread

Yield: 9 x 13-inch pan

3 cups Bisquick®
1 cup sugar
½ cup cornmeal
½ teaspoon salt
1 teaspoon baking powder
1½ cups milk
3 eggs
¾ cup oil
1 tablespoon vanilla
½ cup (1 block) butter

Mix dry ingredients. Add the remaining ingredients, except the butter. Pour into 9 x 13-inch pan and bake at 350°F for 35 minutes or longer until done. Melt butter and spread over top immediately after baking.

Note: This is a buttery and moist cornbread recipe. A family favorite.

Two-Bite Easy Scones

Yield: 24 two-bite scones

1²/₃ cups flour
¼ cup sugar
1½ teaspoons baking powder
½ teaspoon salt
½ cup chopped cranberries
1 cup heavy cream (whipping cream)

Heat oven to 425°F. Mix all dry ingredients, including cranberries. Slowly add cream and mix. Spoon out onto lightly greased cookie sheet to make 24 small scones. Bake for 15 minutes.

Note: Another tasty recipe from Gwen Amai Murai's recipe collection.

Alice's Famous Biscuits

Yield: 24 servings

½ cup (1 block) butter
6 cups flour
¾ cup sugar
4 tablespoons baking powder
4 eggs, slightly beaten
2 cups milk

Preheat oven 400°F. While oven is preheating, place butter in 9 x 13-inch pan and place in oven to melt. When butter melts remove from oven and set aside.

In large bowl, mix together flour, sugar, and baking powder. Add eggs and milk and mix together until just blended. Scoop dough using large spoon and place in pan. Bake for 25 to 30 minutes until brown. Check for doneness. Cut into desired portions.

Hint: Delicious just by itself but it also makes a great strawberry short-cake.

Note: Recipe shared by Alice Ichinose. Alice's husband, Gary, is my classmate (Hilo High School 1957).

Super Easy Popovers

Yield: 12 popovers

    2 eggs
    1 cup cold milk
    1 cup Gold Medal Wondra® quick mixing flour
    1 teaspoon salt

Preheat oven 450°F. Generously grease muffin pan.

Beat eggs with a fork and add milk; beat together. Mix in flour and salt; mix until lumps are gone. Pour into greased muffin pan. Bake at 450°F for 20 to 25 minutes, or until browned. Then reduce oven to 350°F; bake 15 minutes more.

Hawaiian Pineapple Mango Bread

Yield: 6 to 8 servings

    2 cups flour
    ¼ cup sugar
    ½ teaspoon salt
    2 teaspoons cinnamon
    2 teaspoons baking soda
    ¾ cup vegetable oil
    3 eggs
    1 (8.25-ounce) can crushed pineapple in heavy syrup
    2 cups diced mango
    ½ cup chopped nuts

Sift together all dry ingredients in large mixing bowl. Mix well and add oil, eggs and pineapple. Beat well. Add mango and nuts; Mix together. Pour into well greased and floured loaf pan. Bake at 350°F for 1 hour, or until skewer inserted in center comes out cleanly.

. . . .

Note: Moist and delicious! The crushed pineapple really tastes great with the mango. I used frozen mango with good results.

Fresh Blueberry Muffins

Yield: 30 muffins

1 cup (2 blocks) butter or margarine, softened
1½ cups sugar
3 cups + 3 tablespoons flour
2¾ teaspoons baking powder
¾ teaspoon salt
¾ teaspoon nutmeg or cinnamon
3 eggs
1 cup + 2 tablespoons milk
¾ teaspoons vanilla
2¾ cups fresh blueberries

Beat together butter and sugar until light and fluffy. In another bowl, sift together flour, baking powder, salt and nutmeg. Starting and ending with an egg, alternate adding eggs and flour mixture to butter mixture, beating until mixed well. Add milk and vanilla and mix together. Stir in blueberries. Pour into paper-lined muffin pans about 5/8 full. Bake at 375°F for 20 minutes or until done. Remove from oven and let sit for a few minutes before turning them out onto a cooling rack.

. . . .

Note: While visiting Hilo, Kay Yanagihara brought over her fresh blueberry muffins. She always bakes a special treat whenever I visit and these muffins were especially fluffy and tasty. I had to ask her for her recipe.

Cocoa Buttercream Frosting

Yield: about 2 cups

6 tablespoons butter, softened
2¹/₃ cups powdered sugar
½ cup Hershey's® cocoa
¹/₃ milk
1 teaspoon vanilla

Beat butter with spoon. Combine powdered sugar and cocoa; add to butter alternately with milk, beating with spoon to spreading consistency. (Add more milk if necessary.) Stir in vanilla.

Note: Very easy to prepare. If needed, powdered sugar and cocoa may be sifted together to remove any lumps. Frosting remains soft and creamy days later.

PIES

Pie Tips

❀ Use a pastry blender to cut in shortening or butter evenly.

❀ Use heat-resistant glass pie plates or dull-finish aluminum pans for light and flaky pies.

❀ A pie crust is easier to make if all ingredients are cool.

❀ Add a minimal amount of liquid to the pastry, or it will become tough.

❀ A teaspoon of vinegar added to pie dough helps make a flaky crust.

❀ For recipes using beaten egg whites, separate eggs when cold and allow whites to come to room temperature. Egg whites reach their highest volume if beaten at room temperature.

❀ Be sure beaters, bowl, etc. are free of oil. Any trace of oil will prevent egg whites from fluffing up.

❀ Do not overbeat egg whites or they will become stiff and dry.

No Fail Pie Crust

1½ cups flour
½ teaspoon salt
1½ teaspoons sugar
2 tablespoons milk
½ cup oil

Put ingredients in bowl; use hand to mix all ingredients to a soft dough. Press firmly against sides and bottom of 9-inch pie and slightly above. Prick here and there. Bake at 400°F for 10 to 15 minutes until light brown.

Note: Double recipe for 9 x 13-inch pan.

Variation: Add chopped macadamia nuts to crust.

Note: Use for any instant pudding pie mix. (And even as a crust for Quiche Larraine.)

Banana Pie

Yield: 8 servings

3 to 4 cups sliced apple bananas (ripe but firm), cut
  into ¼–inch slices
1 cup pineapple juice
½ cup sugar
3 tablespoons flour
1 teaspoon cinnamon
½ teaspoon nutmeg
Pinch salt
1 tablespoon butter
2 tablespoons milk
Soak sliced bananas in pineapple juice 20 to 30 minutes.

"Easy Pie Crust" (Make 2):
1½ cups flour
½ teaspoon salt
1½ teaspoons sugar
½ cup oil
2 tablespoons milk

While bananas are soaking, prepare bottom crust. Sift together flour, salt and sugar into ungreased 9-inch pie pan. Whip oil and milk with fork until cloudy; pour over flour mixture. Mix with fork until blended. Press dough into pie pan. Set aside.

In mixing bowl, prepare another "Easy Pie Crust" for top crust. Set aside.

Preheat oven to 400°F.

Drain bananas, reserving juice for another use. Combine sugar, flour, cinnamon, nutmeg and salt; mix with bananas. Pour filling into pre-pared pie pan. Crumble second "Easy Pie Crust" evenly over banana filling. Dot with butter and dab lightly with milk. Bake for 30 to 35 minutes. Serve warm or cold.

Suggestion: Mix together 1 teaspoon sugar and ¼ teaspoon cinnamon; sprinkle over top crust before baking for added flavor.

Note: Very delicious! I received a banana pie recipe from Wendy Calizar and also one from Ruby Saito who got it from Pam Honbo. Ruby used the "Easy Pie crust" recipe which eliminated rolling out pie crusts which makes the pie much easier to prepare.

Another option is to use Marie Callender's® frozen 2 Deep Dish Pie Shells. Follow baking directions. This is the easiest of all.

Crumb Crust

Yield: Crust for 1 (9-inch) pie pan

1¼ cups fine crumbs (e.g. graham crackers,
   about 14 rectangle pieces)
3 tablespoons sugar
⅓ cup butter, melted

Combine ingredients and mix well. Press firmly over bottom and sides of 9-inch pie pan or bottom of 8-inch square pan. Chill for 1 hour or bake at 375°F for 8 minutes. Cool before filling. Fill with ice cream, chiffon or cream fillings.

Note: For 8-inch pie pan, reduce crumbs to 1 cup and sugar to 2 tablespoons.

Suggestion: Substitute graham cracker crumbs with chocolate wafers or gingersnaps.

Liliko'i Pistachio Pie

Yield: 10 x 14-inch pan

Crust:
3 cups flour
3½ tablespoons sugar
1⅛ teaspoons salt
1 cup salad oil
3 tablespoons milk + 1 teaspoon milk

Mix all together. Press in 10 x 14-inch pan. Prick shell. Bake at 325°F for 45 minutes until golden brown. Cool.

First Layer:
1½ cups powdered sugar, sifted
2 (8-ounce) packags cream cheese, softened
2 cups Cool Whip®

Beat sugar and cream cheese. Stir in Cool Whip®. Spread on crust. Refrigerate until set.

Second Layer:
2 (3¾-ounce) boxes instant pistachio pudding
3 cups whole milk

Follow directions on box label. Spread over first layer. Refrigerate.

Third Layer:
6 eggs, separated
1 cup fresh liliko'i juice
½ cup cold water
1⅓ cups sugar, divided use
2 packages gelatin

Soak gelatin in water. Beat egg yolks until light. Add 1 cup sugar and continue beating until light. Cook in double boiler, stirring continuously until thick. Remove from heat; add soft gelatin. Beat and cool to room temperature. Add liliko'i juice. Chill to partly set. Whip egg whites until stiff. Add remaining ¹/₃ cup sugar slowly while beating. Fold into whipped gelatin. Mix and pour into baked sheet.

Topping:
1 (8-ounce) container Cool Whip®
Macadamia nuts, finely chopped for sprinkling

Note: This recipe is my sister-in-law's absolute favorite dessert. It was shared by her friends, Warren and Raynette Dang, and is also their family's most requested recipe.

Hint #1: Buy 1 quart whole milk and use for crust and instant pistachio pudding. Do not use skim milk for the instant pistachio pudding.

#2: Refrigerate egg whites until ready to use.

#3. 8-ounce Cool Whip® is about 2½ cups.

Pear Dessert

Yield: 24 servings

Crust:
1 cup (2 blocks) butter, softened
2 tablespoons sugar
1½ cups flour
1 cup finely chopped macadamia nuts

Beat butter and sugar until light and fluffy. Add flour and mix with heavy spoon; mix in nuts. Spread and press in bottom of 9 x 13-inch pan. Bake at 350°F for 20 minutes or till golden brown. Remove from oven and set aside to cool.

Filling:
2 (8-ounce) boxes cream cheese, softened
½ cup sugar
1 teaspoon vanilla
2 eggs

Beat together cream cheese and sugar and vanilla. Add eggs; beat together to blend thoroughly. Spread over cooled crust.

Topping:
3 (15.25-ounce) cans sliced pears, drained
1 teaspoon cinnamon

Slice slightly thicker pear pieces and place pear slices evenly on cream cheese filling. Sprinkle cinnamon on top. Bake at 375°F for 25 to 30 minutes. Cut while warm. Cool and refrigerate.

Fresh Strawberry Pie

Yield: 18-24 pieces

Crust:
1 cup (2 blocks) butter or margarine
4 tablespoons powdered sugar
2 cups flour
½ cup chopped macadamia nuts (optional)

Soften butter to room temperature; mix in sugar, then flour. Add nuts and press evenly into 9 x 13-inch pan. Chill for 30 minutes. Bake at 350°F for 15 minutes or until brown. Cool.

Filling:
2 cups sugar
¼ cup cornstarch
3½ cups water
dash of salt
2 (3-ounce) packages strawberry Jell-O®
2 teaspoons vanilla
1 envelope unflavored gelatin dissolved in 1½ tablespoons
   water
2 (16-ounce) containers strawberries, washed,
   drained, stems and caps removed
1 (8-ounce) container Cool Whip®

Combine sugar, cornstarch, water, and salt in saucepan; cook over medium heat until thickened and clear, stirring constantly. Just before removing from heat, add Jell-O®, vanilla, and gelatin. Set aside and cool thoroughly. Arrange sliced strawberries on cooled crust, reserving some for garnish. Pour cooled filling mixture over fruit. Refrigerate until set, about 3 to 4 hours. Top with whipped topping or sweetened whipped cream. Garnish with strawberries.

Variation: Add sliced bananas to the strawberry mixture.

Lemon Meringue Pie

Yield: 8 servings

1 (9-inch) baked pie shell
1¾ cups sugar
¼ cup cornstarch
3 tablespoons flour
¼ teaspoon salt
2 cups water
4 egg yolks, slightly beaten
⅓ cup lemon juice (about 2 lemons)
Grated rind of 2 lemons
1 tablespoon butter

Combine dry ingredients in medium saucepan. Add water slowly, stirring constantly. Cook on medium heat until thick. Quickly stir some of the hot mixture into egg yolks. Pour back into hot mixture, stir to blend. Add lemon juice and rind and continue cooking 2 minute or more until thick and smooth. Add butter and blend. Cool, stirring occasionally. Pour into baked pie shell. Set aside. Preheat oven to 325°F.

Meringue:
4 egg whites
¼ teaspoon cream of tartar
½ cup sugar

Beat egg whites and cream of tartar at medium speed until frothy. Gradually beat in sugar, beating well after each addition of sugar. Beat at high speed until stiff peaks form when beater is turned off and slowly raised. Spread meringue on pie, carefully sealing to edge of crust. Bake at 325°F for 15 minutes. Cool completely on rack for 2 to 3 hours. Refrigerate, cut with wet knife.

Lemon Pie in Meringue Shell

Yield: 6 to 8 servings

3 egg whites
¼ teaspoon cream of tartar
1½ cups sugar, divided
4 egg yolks
3 tablespoons lemon juice
1 tablespoon grated lemon peel
⅛ teaspoon salt
2 cups heavy whipping cream

Place egg whites in small bowl; let stand at room temperature for 30minutes. Add cream of tartar; beat until soft peaks form. Gradually add 1 cup of the sugar, 1 tablespoon at a time, beating until stiff peaks form. Spread onto bottom and up the sides of a greased 9-inch pie plate. Bake at 350°F for 25 to 30 minutes. Cool on wire rack.

In large saucepan, combine egg yolks, lemon juice, lemon peel, salt and remaining ½ cup sugar. Cook and stir over medium heat until mixture reaches 160°F or is thick enough to coat the back of a metal spoon. Reduce heat and cook and stir 2 minutes longer. Remove from heat. Cool to room temperature without stirring.

In medium bowl, beat whipping cream. Fold half of the whipped cream into lemon filling. Spread into meringue shell. Top with remaining whipped cream. Refrigerate overnight before serving.

Note: Jeri Barnes absolutely loves this pie! Her friend brought this pie over and after tasting it she requested her friend bake it again. She shared the recipe with me with the stipulation that I bake it and invite her over for coffee.

Lemon Chiffon Pie

Yield: 24 servings

Crust:
¾ cup butter (1½ blocks), softened
2 tablespoons powdered sugar
1½ cups flour
¾ cup chopped nuts

Beat butter and sugar until light and fluffy; add flour and mix with wooden spoon until blended. Mix in nuts. Press into 9 x 13-inch pan. Bake at 425°F for 10 minutes or until golden brown. Cool.

Filling:
8 egg yolks, beaten
1 cup sugar
1 cup lemon juice (about 3 large juicy lemons)
1 teaspoon salt
1 cup water
2 envelopes unflavored gelatin
2 tablespoons grated lemon peel

Combine egg yolks, sugar, lemon juice and salt in double boiler and cook on low heat, stirring constantly, until thick. Remove from heat and beat on low speed to blend. Blend gelatin with 1 cup water and add to mixture; stir until gelatin dissolves. Add lemon peel and cool in refrigerator until partially set (30 to 45 minutes).

Topping:
8 egg whites
1 cup sugar
1 cup whipped cream

Beat egg whites until stiff. Then gradually beat in sugar. Fold into cooled mixture. Pour into prepared crust. Chill until firm. Top with whipped cream.

Liliko'i Chiffon Pie

Yield: one 9-inch pie

1 (9-inch) baked pie shell
1 cup sugar, divided use
1 envelope Knox® gelatin
Pinch salt
4 eggs, separated (yolks at room temperature, whites
   in refrigerator)
¼ cup water
½ cup fresh liliko'i juice
Cool Whip® for garnish or topping (about half of
   8-ounce container)

Mix together ½ cup of the sugar, gelatin and salt; set aside.

In medium bowl, beat egg yolks until light and slightly frothy. Add water and liliko'i juice to yolks; beat. Add sugar and gelatin mixture; mix together. Transfer to saucepan and cook over medium heat, stirring constantly, until thick and bubbles begin to appear. Set aside to cool.

Beat egg whites on high until soft peaks form. Add remaining ½ cup sugar gradually. Continue beating until stiff. Fold gently into liliko'i mixture. Pour into pie shell. Chill and top with Cool Whip®.

. . . .

Note: Ruby Saito, who shared this recipe, said, "Many years ago, I got this recipe from my friend, Joyce Hayashi. She learned to make this pie growing up on Kaua'i. Whenever I am able to get fresh liliko'i juice, I use this recipe. It never fails."

Avocado Chiffon Pie

Yield: 8 servings

1 (9-inch) baked pie crust
3 eggs, separated (whites in refrigerator)
¾ cup sugar, divided use
1½ tablespoons butter
1 envelope Knox® gelatin
¼ cup water
1 cup mashed avocado
Cool Whip® for topping (about half of 8-ounce
    container)

In saucepan, cook egg yolks, ¼ cup of the sugar and butter on medium low, stirring constantly, until slightly thick (about 5 minutes). Remove from heat. Dissolve gelatin in water; stir into hot mixture until blended. Transfer to large mixing bowl.

When mixture is slightly cooled, stir in avocado. Set aside.

In medium bowl, beat egg whites until soft peaks form. Add remaining ½ cup sugar gradually. Continue beating until stiff. Fold gently into avocado mixture. Pour into pie shell. Chill and top with Cool Whip®.

. . . .

Note: This recipe is definitely for avocado lovers. Ruby Saito's Aunty Elaine Komo from Kona shared this great recipe.

Tips: Ruby used the "Easy Pie Crust" recipe on page 66 and she said that works well with this pie. I used "Aunty Sarah's Pie Pastry" recipe on page 77 and that worked well, too.

Aunty Sarah's Pie Pastry

Yield: 1 pie crust

1½ cups flour
2 teaspoons sugar
½ teaspoon salt
½ cup cold Crisco®
3 to 4 tablespoons cold water

Sift together flour, sugar and salt. Cut Crisco® into dry ingredients. Add cold water, a tablespoon at a time. Gently toss with fork and knead gently to form a round ball. Let rest for ½ hour.

Place ball on waxed paper over a floured board and flatten ball slightly. Cover ball with another waxed paper and roll between the two pieces of waxed paper. Carefully remove rolled out dough and place in pan; flute edges. Prick bottom and sides well with fork. (Do not prick pastry if filling and crust are to be baked together.) Bake at 425°F for 15 to 20 minutes or until brown. Watch to see that crust does not burn.

. . . .

Note: Thanks to Agnes Leong who shared Aunty Sarah's pie pastry.

Tips: Always roll spoke-fashion, going from center to edge of dough using light strokes. If edges split, pinch together.

Banana Cream Delight

Crust:
1½ cups flour
¾ cup (1½ blocks) cold butter or margarine
1 cup finely chopped macadamia nuts

Blend flour and butter with pastry blender. Mix in ¾ cup of the nuts, reserving ¼ cup to sprinkle. Press into 9 x 13-inch pan. Bake at 350°F for 25 minutes, or until golden brown. Cool.

Middle Layer:
1 (8-ounce) package cream cheese
½ to 1 cup powdered sugar
½ (12-ounce) container of Cool Whip®
4 to 5 bananas (more if desired)

Beat cream cheese and powdered sugar until blended and smooth. Mix in Cool Whip®. Spread over cooled crust. Slice bananas evenly over cream cheese layer. (Make double layer of bananas, if desired.)

Top Layer:
2 (3-ounce) packages instant vanilla pudding
3 cups cold milk
Remaining Cool Whip®

Whip pudding with milk and spread over bananas. Be sure to seal all edges. Spread remaining Cool Whip® on top. Sprinkle with reserved macadamia nuts Refrigerate. Chill several hours to set before serving.

Note: Outstanding! My all-time favorite.

Custard Pie

Yield: 8 servings

4 eggs, slightly beaten
½ cup sugar
¼ teaspoon salt
1 teaspoon vanilla
2½ cups milk, scalded
1 (9-inch) unbaked pie shell
Dash nutmeg

Preheat oven to 475°F. Thoroughly mix together eggs, sugar, salt and vanilla. Slowly add scalded milk to mixture, mixing to blend. Place unbaked pie shell on baking sheet on middle rack. Slowly pour mixture into pie shell. Sprinkle nutmeg over. Bake at 475°F for 5 minutes. Reduce heat to 425°F and bake 10 minutes longer or until knife inserted about halfway comes out cleanly. (Check middle and side.)

Note: When Jennie Tyau's grandson was about 12 years old, he learned how to make this easy custard pie from Jennie. He was able to memorize the ingredients and would bake it often. Jennie gave me this recipe after my cooking demo at a meeting of the O'ahu Retired Teachers' Association.

Magic Crust Custard Pie

Yield: 8 servings

¼ cup butter, softened
¾ cup sugar
4 eggs
2 cups 2% milk
½ cup flour
2 teaspoons vanilla
Pinch salt
Nutmeg for sprinkling

Preheat oven 350°F. Butter a 9-inch, deep dish pie pan; set aside.

Beat together butter, sugar and eggs until just blended. Add milk, flour, vanilla and salt; blend. Place pie pan on oven shelf. Carefully pour custard filling into pie pan. Sprinkle with nutmeg. Bake for 45 minutes.

Note: The flour will settle to make its own crust. Delicious! Best served warm. Pie and recipe were shared by Kelly Goodin who enjoys baking and often shares her treats with my family.

Suggestion For A Quick And Easy Preparation: Kelly put all the ingredients (except for nutmeg) into a blender. Blend for 30 seconds. Pour custard filling into pie pan. Continue with above directions.

Fresh Mango Pie

Yield: 24 to 30 servings

Crust:
2 cups sifted flour
1 cup (2 blocks) butter or margarine
½ cup walnuts, chopped

Cut butter into flour until mixture clings together. Add nuts. Press into 9 x 13-inch pan. Bake at 350°F for 20 to 25 minutes. Cool.

Cream Cheese Filling:
1 (8-ounce) package cream cheese
½ cup powdered sugar
1 teaspoon vanilla
1 (8-ounce) container Cool Whip®

Mix cream cheese and sugar well; add vanilla. Fold mixture into Cool Whip®. Pour over crust. Refigerate.

Topping:
2 envelopes Knox® gelatin
1 cup cold water
1 cup boiling water
1 cup sugar, or less
¼ teaspoon salt
4 tablespoons lemon juice
yellow food coloring, 2 to 3 drops
4 to 5 cups firm, ripe mangoes, chopped (about 8 Hayden mangoes)

Sprinkle gelatin over 1 cup cold water to soften. Add boiling water, sugar, and salt; stir until thoroughly dissolved. Add lemon juice and food coloring; stir to combine. Cool. Add mangoes and chill until gelatin begins to mold. Spoon over cream cheese filling. Refrigerate until firm.

Orange Cream Dessert
Yield: 24 servings

Crust:
¾ cups (1½ blocks) butter
¼ cup brown sugar
1½ cups flour
½ cup chopped nuts

Beat butter and sugar. Add flour and nuts; mix well. Spread into 9 x 13-inch pan. Bake at 375°F for 10 minutes or until golden brown. Cool.

Filling:
1 (8-ounce) box cream cheese, softened
¾ cup sugar
½ (8-ounce) container Cool Whip®

Beat cream cheese and sugar. Fold in Cool Whip®. Spread filling evenly on crust. Chill 30 minutes.

Topping:
1 envelope unflavored Knox® gelatin
1 cup water, divided
1 (6-ounce) package orange Jell-O®
2 cups hot water
2 cups orange sherbet, remove from freezer to begin
    thawing
2 (11-ounce) cans mandarin oranges, drained

Soften unflavored gelatin in ¼ cup of the water; set aside. In large bowl, dissolve Jell-O® with 2 cups hot water; add softened gelatin and remaining ¾ cup water. Stir until dissolved. Stir in Mandarin oranges and sherbet. Ladle mixture over cream cheese filling. Refrigerate.

Note: Very light and refreshing taste.

Chocolate Haupia Pie

Yield: 24 servings

Crust:
1 cup (2 blocks) butter, chilled
2 cups flour
4 tablespoons sugar
½ cup chopped nuts

Filling:
3 (13.5-ounce) cans coconut milk
1¼ cups water
2 cups sugar
½ cup Nestlé® cooking cocoa
13 tablespoons cornstarch
¼ teaspoon salt
1 tablespoon coconut extract

Cut butter into flour and sugar; add nuts and press into 9 x 13-inch pan. Bake at 350°F for 30 minutes. Set aside to cool.

Combine coconut milk and water in pot. Cook on medium heat until small bubbles appear around sides of pot. Stir often to avoid burning. Add sugar, cocoa, cornstarch and salt. Stir constantly until mixture starts to bubble and cook about 8 minutes more, stirring and scraping sides constantly. Remove from stove and add coconut extract. Pour over crust. Cool about 5 to 10 minutes and cover with waxed paper directly on mixture to avoid cracks. Refrigerate until firm.

Note: Delicious! This is a favorite party dessert. If desired, add a squirt of whipped cream over each serving.

Okinawan Sweet Potato Pie with Haupia Topping

Crust:
¾ cup margarine or butter (1½ blocks)
4 tablespoons sugar
1½ cups flour
½ cup chopped nuts (optional)

Combine sugar, flour and nuts. Cut margarine into flour mixture until texture is sandy. Press lightly into 9 x 13-inch pan. Bake at 325°F for 20 to 25 minutes.

Filling:
8 tablespoons butter or margarine, softened
1 cup sugar
2 eggs, beaten
2 cups cooked and mashed Okinawan sweet potato
½ cup evaporated milk
1 teaspoon vanilla
¼ teaspoon salt

Beat butter and sugar. Add eggs and mix. Gradually mix in mashed sweet potatoes. Add evaporated milk, vanilla and salt; mix well. Pour onto crust. Bake at 350°F for 30 to 35 minutes. Cool.

Haupia topping:
½ cup sugar
½ cup cornstarch
1½ cups water
2 (12-ounce) cans coconut milk

Combine sugar and cornstarch; stir in water and blend well. Stir sugar mixture into coconut milk; cook and stir over low heat until thickened. Cool slightly. Pour coconut-milk mixture (haupia) over pie filling and refrigerate.

Note: A new favorite that combines the different textures of a light crust, dense sweet potato and smooth haupia. A hands-down winner at any gathering.

Tofu Pie

1 Keebler Ready Crust® (butter pie crust or graham)
1 (3-ounce) package lemon Jell-O®
1 cup boiling water
1 to 2 tablespoons lemon juice
½ teaspoon lemon extract
½ (20-ounce) container tofu, smooth/soft type
½ (8-ounce) container Cool Whip®

Mix together Jell-O®, boiling water, lemon juice and lemon extract. Refrigerate until slightly firm. Drain tofu. Blend tofu and Cool Whip® in Osterizer® or use electric mixer. Mix in Jell-O® mixture. Pour into crust. Refrigerate. When firm, garnish with kiwi fruit or any canned fruit.

Variation: Substitute strawberry Jell-O® for lemon Jell-O®. Garnish with sliced fresh strawberries.

Note: You must try this! Tofu is blended and mixed and transformed into a smooth refreshing dessert. No one will know it's tofu. My daughter, Cheryl, always has raves on this pie.

Variation: To make individual tarts, use small graham cracker cupcake-size containers.

Note: Pie will still be soft; be careful when taking pie out of oven. Cool for several hours to harden. Need not be refrigerated.

Haupia Cream Cheese Pie

Crust:
2 cups (about 24 crackers) crushed graham crackers
1 cup (2 blocks) butter, melted

Grind or crush graham crackers into crumbs. Mix with melted butter and press into 9 x 13-inch pan. Refrigerate.

Cream Cheese Filling:
2 (8-ounce) packages cream cheese, softened
1½ cups powdered sugar, sifted
1 teaspoon vanilla
2 cups Cool Whip®

Beat cream cheese and sugar; add vanilla. Stir in Cool Whip®. Spread on crust. Refrigerate until set.

Haupia:
3 (12-ounce) cans coconut milk
1¼ cups sugar
1¼ cups cornstarch

In a saucepan, mix all ingredients until smooth. Cook on medium heat, stirring continuously, until mixture thickens. Remove from heat and cool down mixture continuing to stir. When cool to touch, pour haupia over cream cheese filling. Refrigerate to set.

Blueberry Cream Cheese Pie

Yield: 24 servings

Crust:
1½ cups flour
¼ cup brown sugar
1 cup (2 blocks) butter
½ cup chopped nuts

Mix together flour and brown sugar. Cut in butter. Mix in nuts. Press into 9 x 13-inch pan. Bake at 350°F for 15 to 20 minutes or until golden brown. Remove from oven. Cool.

Filling:
1 cup whipping cream (e.g. Meadow Gold® Whipping Cream)
1 (8-ounce) box cream cheese, softened
¾ cup powdered sugar, sifted
1 teaspoon vanilla
1 (21-ounce) can blueberry pie filling

Beat whipping cream until peaks form; set aside.

In large bowl beat together cream cheese, sugar and vanilla. Fold whipped cream into cream cheese mixture; spread over crust. Top with blueberry pie filling. Chill for 2 hours or longer before serving.

Note: Okay, Cheryl, this is for you. You requested Grandma Watanabe's blueberry recipe and here it is. It has less cream cheese and uses fresh whipping cream instead of Cool Whip®. Grandma's original recipe called for Avoset® whipping cream which is no longer on the shelves.

Cream Cheese Pumpkin Pie

Yield: 24 servings

Crust:
¾ cup (1½ blocks) butter, softened
¼ cup brown sugar
1½ cups flour
½ cup nuts, chopped

Beat butter and brown sugar; add flour and blend. Mix in nuts. Spread evenly in 11 x 14-inch pan. Partially bake at 350°F for about 7 to 10 minutes. Remove; set aside.

Cream Cheese Layer:
2 (8-ounce) boxes cream cheese, softened
½ cup sugar
1 teaspoon vanilla
2 eggs

Beat cream cheese; add sugar and beat together. Add vanilla and eggs. Mix well. Spread evenly over partially baked crust.

Filling:
4 eggs, slightly beaten
1 (29-ounce) can pumpkin
1½ cups sugar
1 teaspoon salt
1 teaspoon cinnamon
¼ teaspoon ginger
¼ teaspoon nutmeg
2 (12-ounce) cans evaporated milk

Increase oven temperature to 425°F. Mix all filling ingredients; carefully ladle over cream cheese mixture, partially filling pan. Carefully place in oven and add more pumpkin filling. Bake at 425°F for 15 minutes, then at 350°F for 45 to 55 minutes. Insert knife to test for doneness. Refrigerate when cool.

Suggestion: Top with Cool Whip® when serving.

Note: This is an old favorite recipe shared by Juliet Morita who taught at Puohala Elementary in the 70s. We all love it.

Jell-O® Cream Cheese Pie

Yield: 24 servings

Crust:
1½ cups flour
¼ cup brown sugar
¾ cup cold butter (1½ blocks)
½ cup chopped nuts

Mix flour and sugar; cut in butter until crumbly. Mix in nuts. Press dough into 9 x 13-inch pan. Bake at 375°F for 10 minutes or until the top browns.

Filling:
1 (3-ounce) box lemon Jell-O®
1 cup hot water
1 (8-ounce) box cream cheese, softened
½ cup sugar
1 cup (½ pint) whipping cream e.g. Meadow Gold®
   Whipping Cream

Dissolve lemon Jell-O® in hot water; set aside to cool. In large bowl, beat cream cheese and sugar together. In medium bowl, whip whipping cream and add to cream cheese mixture; blend. Add cooled Jell-O®; blend and pour over cooled crust. Chill until firm (preferably overnight).

Topping:
2 (3-ounce) boxes Jell-O®, any desired flavor
3 cups hot water

Dissolve Jell-O® in hot water. Cool. Pour over cream cheese mixture, slowly and carefully. Chill until firm before serving.

Peanut Butter Cream Cheese Chocolate Pie

Crust:
2 cups (about 24 crackers) crushed graham cracker
1 cup (2 blocks) butter, melted

Grind or crush graham crackers into crumbs. Mix with melted butter and press into 9 x 13-inch pan. Refrigerate.

Cream Cheese Filling:
3 (8-ounce) packages cream cheese
2 (8-ounce) containers Cool Whip®
1¼ cups powdered sugar, sifted
1 tablespoon vanilla
½ cup peanut butter

Mix all ingredients. Layer over crust. Refrigerate.

Pudding Topping:
4 (3.4-ounce) boxes cook-and-serve chocolate pudding
6 cups milk

Combine pudding mix and milk. Cook on medium heat, stirring constantly until mixture is thick and bubbles appear. Remove from heat and cool, continuing to mix so "skin" doesn't form. When cool to touch, pour pudding over cream cheese filling. Refrigerate to set.

Note: A fantastic high cream cheese pie with a taste of peanut butter topped off with a generous chocolate pudding. Thank you, Keith, for sharing this recipe with me.

Chocolate Delight

Crust:
1½ cups flour
¾ cup (1½ blocks) butter or margarine
½ cup chopped walnuts or macadamia nuts

Blend flour and butter with pastry blender. Mix in nuts. Press lightly into 9 x 13-inch pan. Bake at 425°F for 10 minutes. Cool.

First Layer:
1 (8-ounce) package cream cheese
1 cup powdered sugar
½ (12-ounce) container Cool Whip®

Beat cream cheese and sugar; mix in Cool Whip® and pour onto cooled crust.

Second Layer:
3 (3-ounce) boxes instant chocolate pudding
4½ cups cold milk

Combine chocolate pudding and milk and beat with wire whisk or electric mixer on lowest speed until thick. Pour over first layer.

Topping:
½ container Cool Whip®

Top with other half of Cool Whip®. Refrigerate for several hours to set before serving.

Variation: For the second layer, substitute 3 cups milk, 2 boxes of coffee instant-pudding mix and 1 teaspoon vanilla.

Pecan Pie

Yield: 6 to 8 servings

1 (9-inch) pie crust, unbaked
1 cup light corn syrup
1 cup dark brown sugar, firmly packed
3 eggs, slightly beaten
1/3 cup butter, melted
½ teaspoon salt
1 teaspoon vanilla
1¼ cups pecan halves

In large bowl, combine corn syrup, sugar, eggs, butter, salt and vanilla; mix well. Pour into unbaked pie crust; sprinkle pecans evenly over.

Bake at 350°F for 50 to 60 minutes or until center is set (may take more time). Insert toothpick in center to check for doneness. Cool.

Note: If pie appears to be getting too brown, cover with foil for the remaining baking time. This pie is delicious! Very rich but great for the Christmas holidays.

Pecan Tarts

Yield: 4 dozen

1 (8-ounce) package cream cheese, softened
1 cup butter or margarine, room temperature
2 cups flour
2 eggs, beaten
1½ cups brown sugar, packed
2 teaspoons vanilla
1½ cups chopped pecans
Powdered sugar, for sprinkling (optional)

Combine cream cheese and butter, mixing until well blended. Add flour, mix well. Divide dough into 4 parts; divide each part into 12 balls. Press each ball onto bottom and sides of miniature muffin pans.

Combine eggs, brown sugar and vanilla; stir in pecans. Spoon into pastry shells, filling each cup. Bake at 325°F for 30 minutes, or until pastry is golden brown. Cool 5 minutes; remove from pans. Sprinkle with powdered sugar, if desired.

Mandarin Peach Cake • pg. 16

Holiday Spice Cake • pg. 38

Miniature Cream Cheesecake • pg. 48

Almond Cookies • pg. 100

Chocolate Crinkle Cookies • pg. 117

©Knelson20 | dreamstime.com

Russian Tea Balls • pg. 122

Ray Wong

Okinawan Sweet Potato Pie with Haupia Topping • pg. 84

Lemon Bars with Poppy Seed Crust • pg. 127

Fresh Blueberry Muffins • pg. 61

Fresh Strawberry Mochi • pg. 155

Rainbow Jell-O® • pg. 161

Carrot Cake • pg. 8

Aggie's Oatmeal Cookies • pg. 116

Pear Dessert • pg. 70

Red Velvet Cupcakes • pg. 47

Jeri's Easy Trifle • pg. 49

Sponge Drops • pg. 121

COOKIES
and Bars

Cookie Tips

❀ For uniform baking, make each cookie the same size and thickness.

❀ Always place dough on a cool cookie sheet.

❀ Bake one sheet of cookies at a time on the center rack. If using 2 sheets, exchange rack positions and rotate sheets halfway through baking time.

❀ Grease cookie sheet only if specified in the recipe.

❀ When specified, grease cookie sheets lightly once before baking, it is not necessary to grease again.

❀ Check cookies at the end of minimum baking time.

❀ Cut bar cookies into bars, squares or triangles when cool unless recipe specifies cutting while warm.

❀ For refrigerator cookies, shape dough firmly into a long smooth roll of the diameter specified in the recipe. Wrap rolled dough in waxed paper or plastic wrap, twisting ends, and chill until firm. Use a thin sharp knife to slice dough.

❀ For drop cookies, use a small ice cream scooper to drop dough on cookie sheet. Or use 2 teaspoons (not measuring spoons), one teaspoon for scooping dough and the other for scraping dough off.

Sugar Cookies

1½ cups sifted powdered sugar
1 cup butter
1 egg
1 teaspoon vanilla
½ teaspoon almond extract
2½ cups flour, sifted
1 teaspoon cream of tarter
1 teaspoon baking soda

Beat sugar and butter; add egg, vanilla and almond extract. Mix thoroughly. Sift flour, cream of tarter and baking soda. Stir into butter mixture and blend together. Refrigerate 2 to 3 hours. Divide dough in half and roll out on lightly floured board. Roll thin but thick enough to pick up the design of the cookie cutters. Dip cutter in flour before each rolling. Cut as many cookies from each rolling as possible. The least amount of working with the dough gives the best cookie. Place on lightly greased baking sheet. Bake at 375°F for 7 to 8 minutes or until delicately golden.

Drop Sugar Cookies

Yield: 3½ dozen cookies

2½ cups flour
¾ teaspoon salt
½ teaspoon baking soda
½ cup (1 block) butter, softened
½ cup Crisco® vegetable shortening, softened
1 cup sugar
1 teaspoon vanilla
1 egg
2 tablespoons milk

Sift flour, salt and baking soda together; set aside.

In large bowl, beat butter, shortening and sugar until light and fluffy. Add egg and vanilla; beat together. Add dry ingredients and beat until smooth. Blend in milk. Drop by tablespoonful about 3 inches apart on greased or parchment-lined cookie sheet. Bake at 350°F for 12 to 15 minutes or until lightly browned.

Note: For crispier cookies, press down slightly and flatten dough before baking.

Suggestion: Decorate with colored icing. (See page 120 for Cookie Icing recipe.)

Lemon Cookies

Yield: 6 dozen

1 cup (2 blocks) butter, softened
1 cup sugar
1 cup powdered sugar
1 cup vegetable oil
2 eggs
1 to 2 teaspoons lemon extract
4¾ cups flour
1 teaspoon baking soda
1 teaspoon salt
1 teaspoon cream of tartar

In large bowl, beat together butter and sugars until creamy. Beat in oil, eggs and lemon extract.

In another bowl, sift together flour, baking soda, salt and cream of tartar. Add to butter mixture and mix together until blended. Refrigerate 1 hour for easier handling. Scoop out rounded teaspoonfuls and roll into balls: place on cookie sheets. Bake at 350°F for 10 to 15 minutes, or until lightly browned.

Note: Ellen Chew's 94 year old sister-in-law makes these cookies and they are so light and airy. They practically melt in your mouth.

Almond Cookies

Yield: 5-½ dozen

1 cup + 3 tablespoons shortening or butter
1 cup sugar
1 egg, beaten
1 teaspoon almond extract
2½ cups flour
½ teaspoon salt
½ teaspoon baking soda
Red food color
Blanched almonds (optional)

Beat shortening and sugar; add egg and almond extract. Mix well. Sift flour, salt and baking soda; add to sugar and egg mixture. Mix well. Shape into walnut-size balls. Place on ungreased cookie sheet. Using thumb, press center of balls to make a depression. Using the end of a chopstick, dip in red food color and place a dot in the center of each cookie. A blanched almond may be pressed into the center if preferred. Bake at 350° for 15 to 18 minutes.

Note: This is an authentic Chinese almond cookie recipe that was shared by Aunty Clara (Chun). The best almond cookie recipe I have tasted.

Macadamia Nut Chocolate Chip Cookies

2¼ cups flour
1 teaspoon baking soda
1 teaspoon salt
1 cup (2 blocks) butter, softened
¾ cup sugar
¾ cup brown sugar, firmly packed
1 teaspoon vanilla
2 eggs
2 cups (one 12-ounce package) semisweet chocolate
    morsels
1 cup macadamia nuts

In small bowl, combine flour, baking soda and salt; set aside. In large bowl, combine butter, sugar, brown sugar and vanilla; beat until light and creamy. Beat in eggs. Gradually add flour mixture. Stir in chocolate morsels and nuts. Drop by level tablespoonfuls onto ungreased cookie sheets. Bake at 375° for 9 to 11 minutes.

Macadamia Nut Butter Cookies

Yield: 6 dozen cookies

1 cup butter or margarine
2/3 cup powdered sugar
1 teaspoon vanilla
2¼ cups flour
¼ teaspoon salt
1½ cups macadamia nut bits

In large bowl, beat butter and sugar. Stir in vanilla. Mix in flour, salt and nuts. Shape into 2 rolls. Chill for 1 hour. Cut rolls into ¼-inch slices. Bake at 350°F for 12 to 15 minutes.

Norma's Cookies

Yield: 6½ dozen

1 pound (4 blocks) butter, softened
1½ cups sugar
1 tablespoon vanilla
4 cups flour
2 teaspoons baking soda

Beat together butter and sugar until light and fluffy. Mix in vanilla. Sift flour and baking soda and add in batches to butter mixture; mix to blend. Select two or three of the following options to add to the batter.

Optional:
1 cup nuts
1 cup oatmeal
1 cup raisins or Craisins®
1 cup chocolate chips
1 cup Rice Krispies®

Scoop out dough and place on cookie sheet. Bake at 325°F for 20 to 25 minutes.

Note: Shared by Ruby Saito who got this delicious crispy recipe from Norma, a 1960 Roosevelt High School classmate. I especially like this recipe because you can make this cookie with whatever you have on hand.

Gingersnap Cookies

Yield: 150 cookies

4½ cups flour
½ teaspoon salt
2½ teaspoons baking soda
2 teaspoons ginger
1½ teaspoons cinnamon
1½ teaspoons cloves
1½ cups Crisco® shortening
1½ cups sugar
2 eggs
½ cup molasses
½ cup sugar for coating

Sift together flour, salt, baking soda, ginger, cinnamon and cloves. Set aside.

In large bowl, beat together shortening, sugar and eggs until light and fluffy (about 2 to 3 minutes). Add molasses; blend. Add dry ingredients in small batches and mix using a spatula or heavy spoon until well blended. Refrigerate overnight.

Form into 1-inch balls and roll the balls of dough into ½ cup sugar. Place, spaced apart, on greased cookie sheet (or cookie sheet lined with parchment paper). Flatten and bake at 350°F for 10 to 15 minutes or until browned. Remove immediately and place on rack to cool.

Note: I tasted Carolyn Inouye's Gingersnap Cookies and they were so tasty and crisp I asked for the recipe. Carolyn is known for her delicious cookies. She uses 5 cookie sheets and fits 30 small cookies on each sheet. Instead of using butter as the original recipe called for, I used shortening for easier handling.

Furikake Arare Cookies

Yield: 3½ dozen

2 cups flour
1 teaspoon baking soda
1 cup (2 blocks) butter, softened
1 cup sugar
1 teaspoon vanilla
¼ cup nori kome furikake
1½ cups mini yakko arare

Sift together flour and baking soda; set aside.

In large mixing bowl, beat together butter and sugar about 2 to 3 minutes until fluffy. Mix in vanilla. Add flour mixture in two batches; mix until dough starts to come together. Do not overmix. Stir in furikake and arare. Cover with plastic wrap and chill dough about 20 minutes in refrigerator.

Preheat oven to 325°F and grease cookie sheets with nonstick cooking spray.

Drop dough by rounded teaspoons or small scoop onto baking sheet. Flatten slightly. Bake 15 to 18 minutes or until golden brown. Remove from oven and cool on cookie sheet about 10 minutes. Transfer cookies to wire rack to cool completely.

Note: You may use any type of arare but pieces larger than mini yakko should be crushed.

Garbage Cookies

Yield: 8 dozen

1 cup (2 blocks) butter, softened to room temperature
1 cup sugar
1 cup brown sugar
2 eggs, beaten
1 teaspoon vanilla
2 cups flour
½ teaspoon baking powder
1 teaspoon baking soda
½ teaspoon salt
2 cups quick oatmeal
2 cups Rice Krispies® cereal
1 cup shredded coconut
1 cup chopped nuts
1 cup chocolate chips

In large bowl beat butter and sugars until creamy. Add eggs and vanilla; beat together.

In separate bowl, sift flour, baking powder, baking soda and salt. Add to butter mixture and mix together.

Mix together oatmeal, Rice Krispies®, coconut, nuts and chocolate chips together; add to batter. Form into balls; press lightly onto ungreased cookie sheet. Bake at 350°F for 12 to 15 minutes.

Note: I met Betty Ikei at Safeway one early morning and we started to discuss recipes. She is such a friendly and generous person. Before I left the store she promised to give me some of her and her family's favorite recipes. Here is one of them. "Garbage Cookies" is an old, old family favorite. Someone must have named it so because of all the different ingredients that go into it.

Granny's Cookies

Yield: 6½ dozen

1¾ cups (3½ sticks) butter
1 cup sugar
1½ teaspoons vanilla
3 cups flour
1¾ teaspoons baking soda
2 cups Rice Krispies®
1 cup Cocoa Krispies®

Beat butter and sugar until creamy. Add vanilla. Sift together flour and baking soda; add to butter mixture in 3 to 4 parts. Fold in Rice and Cocoa Krispies®. Drop by teaspoonfuls on cookie sheet. Bake at 275° for 35 to 40 minutes.

. . . .

Variation: Substitute Cocoa Krispies® with package of chocolate chips.

Note: Very crispy and light. Everyone's favorite! If rushed, bake at 325°F for 15 minutes.

Note: Great raves! Very light, crispy and crunchy. A local favorite!

Gingerbread Cookies

Yield: 14 to 15 gingerbread men

2¼ blocks margarine, softened*
1½ cups sugar
½ cup molasses
2 small eggs, or medium eggs
5¼ cups flour
3 teaspoons baking soda
1¼ teaspoon cloves
1¼ teaspoon ginger
2 teaspoons cinnamon
½ teaspoon salt
Raisins, M&M's®, chocolate chips, icing, etc. to decorate

In large bowl, beat margarine and sugar until creamy. Add molasses; beat well. Add eggs, one at a time; beat well.

In another bowl, sift dry ingredients together and add to margarine mixture in small batches. Beat with beater on low speed. Mix with spatula or heavy spoon as dough thickens. Refrigerate 2 hours or overnight.

After refrigeration, form into 14 to 15 balls, about the size of a small orange. (If dough still seems too soft to handle, try sprinkling and mixing in more flour.) Refrigerate balls of dough until ready to use.

* Do not use Imperial® margarine or butter. Dough becomes too soft.

Making Gingerbread Men with Children:

Provide a foil about 9-inches wide for each child. Use a permanent marker to write each child's name at the top in the middle of the foil. Give each child a ball of dough and have him follow your directions to create his own gingerbread man.

Divide the ball of dough into 4 parts. Roll into smooth balls.

Select the smallest piece for the gingerbread man's head. Form into a ball and place it directly under child's name. Press very firmly to flatten. (Flatten as much as possible to get a firmer cookie.)

For the body, select the largest piece. Shape into an oval and place it overlapping where the chin should be. Press to flatten.

Select the third piece and roll into stick shape. Break in half and press flat on body where arms should be. Do the same with last piece for the legs. Be sure to overlap and press each piece firmly onto body.

Decorate with raisins to make a mouth, M&M's® for eyes, chocolate chips, icing, etc.

Place each gingerbread man on foil onto cookie sheet. Trim or fold corners of foil to fit better. Bake at 375°F for 10 to 12 minutes or until done. Cool and give each child the gingerbread man he created. Each gingerbread man will be approximately 5 inches tall equivalent to 4 cookies.

This is a great activity for children and even for teenagers and certainly not limited to gingerbread men. Teenagers can be very creative. Any left-over dough can be rolled out on parchment paper, cut out with a cookie cutter and baked on parchment-lined cookie pans.

Note: I did this activity with my kindergarten classes involving parents. Great fun and a great learning experience! One batch was done the night before. The second recipe was done at school in the morning with the children, refrigerated, and ready for each child to make his own gingerbread man in the afternoon.. The cookies were baked with help from the cafeteria staff. The children were so proud of their creations!

Spice Shortbread Cookies

Yield: 8½ dozen

1 pound (4 blocks) butter, softened
1¼ cup sugar
2 teaspoons vanilla
5 cups flour
2 to 3 teaspoons cinnamon
½ to ¾ teaspoon nutmeg
¼ teaspoon allspice (optional)

Beat butter and sugar until creamy; mix in vanilla. In another bowl, sift together flour, cinnamon, nutmeg and allspice, if desired. Add to butter mixture in small batches; using a spatula or heavy spoon, mix well.

Form into ¾- to 1-inch round balls. Place on ungreased cookie sheets and flatten to about ¼-inch thick or less. Prick several times with a fork and bake at 350°F for 14 to 18 minutes or until golden tan or brown. (The longer you bake, the crispier the cookies will be.)

Note: This is Jean Machida Bart's creation based on a recipe from Elaine Inouye. She was so generous to share it with us.

Tip: Jean uses 3 trays at once in her convection oven which automatically reduces the temperature about 25°F. It takes from 22 to 28 minutes. I used a regular oven with a single tray and baked it for 17 minutes.

M&M® Cookies

Yield: 12 dozen

2 cups (4 blocks) butter, softened
2 cups brown sugar
1 cup sugar
4 eggs
1 tablespoon vanilla
4½ cups flour
2 teaspoons baking soda
1 teaspoon salt
2 cups (one 12.60-ounce bag) milk chocolate M&M's®
   candies

Beat butter and sugar until light and fluffy. Beat in eggs and vanilla until thoroughly blended. Sift dry ingredients together. Gradually add sifted dry ingredients to butter mixture; blend together. Stir in M&M's® into cookie dough. Drop by teaspoonful onto lightly greased baking ,sheets. Bake at 350°F for 13 to 15 minutes.

Potato Chip Cookies

Yield: 3½ dozen

1 cup (2 blocks) unsalted butter
½ cup sugar
Dash vanilla
1¾ cups flour
1¼ cups crushed potato chips
Powdered sugar for sprinkling (optional)

In large bowl, beat together butter and sugar until light and fluffy. Beat in vanilla. Add flour; blend. Mix in crushed potato chips. Chill for 30 minutes to firm dough for handling. Roll into 1-inch balls; place on cookie sheets and press down with a fork dipped in flour. Bake at 350°F for 15 minutes or until edges are brown. Sprinkle with powdered sugar.

Note: Very light and tasty with a slight crunch. (I placed 3 cookies in a cupcake baking cup wrapped them prettily and they were perfect for a little luncheon favor for a group of friends,) I also liked the cookies baked without pressing down, something like Russian Tea Cookies.

Oatmeal Crisp Cookies

Yield: 6½ dozen

1 cup (2 blocks) butter, softened
1¼ cups sugar
2 egg yolks
2 cups flour
2 teaspoons baking soda
1¼ cups quick oatmeal
1 (12-ounce) bag semi-sweet chocolate chips or use
    less (about 1½ cups)
¾ cup macadamia nut bits

Beat butter and sugar until creamy; add egg yolks and beat together. Sift flour with baking soda and stir into batter. Add oatmeal and chocolate chips into batter. Add nuts; mix together. Roll into one inch balls (Do not flatten.) Place onto cookie sheets. Bake at 345°F for 10 to 15 minutes or until brown. Remove from oven and let cool on sheets slightly before removing.

Note: These cookies are really yummy and flaky! Be sure to use butter, not margarine.

Note: Gwen Murai shared these delicious cookies at one of our Hilo High Class of '57 luncheons. She says you can leave the cookies in the oven longer if you want them browner and crispier. She begins with the 1st tray on the lower rack for 5 minutes or so until cookies expand. Then she moves it to the upper rack and puts the 2nd tray on the lower rack, etc.

Peanut Butter Cookies

Yield: 7 dozen

1 cup (2 blocks) butter, softened
1 cup creamy peanut butter
1 cup sugar
1 cup packed brown sugar
2 eggs
2½ cups flour
1 teaspoon baking powder
1½ teaspoons baking soda
½ teaspoon salt (or use less)

In large bowl beat together butter, peanut butter, sugars. Add eggs and beat together thoroughly; set aside.

In another bowl, sift together flour, baking powder, baking soda and salt (dry ingredients). Add dry ingredients into butter mixture and mix thoroughly with wooden spoon. Chill dough for about one hour in refrigerator. Take out a small amount of chilled dough and roll dough into balls the size of large walnuts. Place onto ungreased baking sheets. Leave room for cookies to expand. Flatten crisscross fashion with fork dipped in flour. Bake at 325°F for 10 to 12 minutes or until brown.

Note: Measure flour by dip-level-pour method. Scoop up flour in measuring cup, level with butter knife sliding across rim and pour into sifter.

Note: Gwen Murai contributed this crispy and tasty peanut butter cookie recipe. This is my favorite peanut butter cookie now!

Peanut Butter Blossoms

Yield: 3½ dozen

½ cup sugar
½ cup brown sugar
½ cup (1 block) butter, softened
½ cup peanut butter
1 egg
1 teaspoon vanilla
¼ teaspoon salt
1¾ cups flour
1 teaspoon baking soda
¼ cup sugar for coating
42 to 48 milk chocolate candy kisses, unwrapped

In large bowl, beat together ½ cup sugar, brown sugar, butter and peanut butter at medium speed until light and fluffy. Add egg, vanilla and salt; continue beating until well mixed. Add flour and baking soda. Beat, scraping bowl often, until well mixed.

Shape dough into 1-inch balls; roll in sugar to coat each cookie. Place onto ungreased cookie sheets about 2 inches apart. Press down slightly with flat surface. Bake at 375°F for 8 to 10 minutes or until golden brown. Remove from oven and immediately press 1 chocolate kiss in center of each cookie. Place on wire racks and cool completely.

Tip: If dough is too soft to shape into balls, refrigerate 30 to 60 minutes.

Note: These cookies are pretty to look at and delicious. A Goodin family favorite. Kids will love them. Storage is a problem as they can't be stacked but they'll disappear quickly.

Aggie's Oatmeal Cookies

Yield: 5 dozen

1 cup (2 blocks) butter, softened
1 cup white sugar
1 cup brown sugar
2 eggs
1 teaspoon vanilla
1½ cups flour
1 teaspoon salt
1 teaspoon baking soda
3 cups oatmeal
1 cup chopped nuts
1 cup raisins

Beat together butter and sugars until smooth and creamy. Add eggs one at a time; beating together. Add vanilla; beat together. In another bowl, sift together flour, salt and baking soda; add to butter mixture and mix together with large spoon or spatula. Add oatmeal, nuts and raisins; mix together. Drop about 1 heaping teaspoonful batter on ungreased cookie sheet and lightly press. Bake at 350°F for about 10 to 15 minutes. Check for doneness.

Suggestion: Bake 15 minutes for crispier cookies.

Note: Aggie often shared her delicious home-baked cookies with others at St. Ann's Church. This was my favorite cookie. Aggie recommends that all ingredients be at room temperature before beginning and she also recommends beating butter and sugars together really well.

Chocolate Crinkle Cookies

Yield: 4½ dozen

2 cups flour
2 teaspoons baking powder
½ teaspoon salt
4 ounces unsweetened chocolate
2 cups sugar
½ cup oil
4 eggs
2 teaspoons vanilla
Powdered sugar for coating

Sift together flour, baking powder and salt; set aside.

Place chocolate in large microwaveable bowl and heat for about 3 minutes to melt. Add sugar and oil; mix together. Blend in one egg at a time until mixed well. Add vanilla and flour mixture; mix well. Chill in refrigerator for several hours or overnight.

When chilled, place powdered sugar in bowl. Drop small teaspoonful of dough into the sugar. Roll and shape into a ball. Place about 2 inches apart on greased cookie sheet or parchment lined cookie sheet. Bake at 350°F for 10 to 12 minutes. As they bake and expand, the cookies will take on a crackly beautiful "snowy" look.

. . . .

Hint: Use 2 teaspoons, one to scoop dough and the other to scrape off dough into powdered sugar. Dough will be easier to handle once it is covered with powdered sugar.

Note: Pauline Masuda shared this recipe which she got from Maureen Beng who has had this recipe for over 40 years.

Cocoa Krispies™ Chocolate Chip Cookies

Yield: 3½ dozen

1 cup (2 blocks) unsalted butter, softened at room
  temperature
¾ cup sugar
1 teaspoon vanilla
2 cups flour, sifted
1 teaspoon baking soda
¼ teaspoon salt
1 cup semisweet chocolate chips
3½ cups chocolate crispy cereal (e.g. Kellogg's® Cocoa
  Krispies)

In large bowl, beat butter, sugar and vanilla on medium low for 2 to 3 minutes. In smaller bowl, combine flour, baking soda and salt; slowly add to butter mixture, beating on medium until blended. With rubber spatula or heavy spoon, mix in chocolate chips. Refrigerate dough 10 to 15 minutes for easier handling.

Scoop dough with teaspoon or small ice cream scooper and roll into a ball about an inch in diameter. Roll in cereal until cookie is wellcovered. Place on ungreased cookie sheet. Place a sheet of waxed paper over cookies and flatten balls slightly using the bottom of a cup or can. Bake at 350°F for 18 to 20 minutes or until golden brown.

Soft Molasses Cookies

Yield: 7 dozen

1¼ cups (2½ blocks) butter, softened
1 cup brown sugar
½ cup honey
2 eggs
1 cup dark molasses
2 teaspoons baking soda
1 teaspoon cinnamon
½ teaspoon ground cloves
1 teaspoon salt
6 cups flour

Beat butter and sugar until creamy; add the rest of ingredients (except for flour) and mix together. Use heavy spoon to mix as you slowly add flour. Dough will be very thick. Chill overnight.

Spoon out large tablespoon of dough, roll into ball, place on ungreasedcookie sheet and flatten with bottom of a glass, dipped in flour. Bake at 350°F about 10 to 15 minutes.

Note: Although cookies were meant to be soft, if you prefer crispier cookies, bake longer.

Suggestion: Decorate with icing. Use store bought icing or use icing recipe on page 120.

Stone Cookies

Yield: 3½ dozen

4 cups flour
2 teaspoons baking soda
1 teaspoon baking powder
½ teaspoon salt
½ cup (1 block) butter, softened
¼ cup oil
1½ cups sugar
3 eggs, beaten
¼ cup milk or water
2 teaspoons vanilla
Sugar for dusting

Sift flour, baking soda, baking powder and salt; set aside.

In large bowl, beat together butter, oil and sugar. Add eggs, milk and vanilla; beat together. Add dry ingredients and mix well. Chill for 1 hour for easier handling. Scoop out rounded tablespoonful of dough. Form into a ball and roll in sugar. Place onto parchment-lined or greased cookie sheet. Flatten with palm. Bake at 325°F for 25 minutes until golden brown and crisp.

....

Note: I also like it not so crispy and on the slightly chewy side. It reminds me of the Chinese soft cookies Goon Goon and Popo used to buy from Chinatown.

Cookie Icing

2 cups powdered sugar, sifted
4 teaspoons milk
4 teaspoons light corn syrup

Blend icing ingredients until smooth. Add more sugar or milk as needed for spreading consistency. Food color may be added, if desired.

Sponge Drops

Yield: 50 small cookies

3 eggs
¾ cup sugar
½ teaspoon cream of tartar
¼ teaspoon baking soda
1 cup + 2 tablespoons sifted cake flour
Parchment paper for cookie sheet

Beat eggs well, until fluffy and light. Add sugar slowly and contin-ue beating. In another bowl, combine sifted flour, baking soda and cream of tartar and sift again. Add into egg mixture and beat well. Let set for 15 to 20 minutes. Carefully drop dough from teaspoon on parchment-lined cookie sheet and bake at 375°F for about 5 min-utes, or until brown. Cool slightly on parchment paper. Use spatula to transfer to cooling rack. Refrigerate. Bake cookies 1 day before adding whipped cream. Refrigerate in covered container.

Whipped Cream:
2 tablespoons powdered sugar
1 teaspoon vanilla
1 cup whipping cream

Beat together sugar, vanilla and cream until whipped. Sprinkle pow-dered sugar on cookies. Top cookies with whipped cream or place two cookies together with whipped cream in the middle.

Variation: Substitute with Cool Whip®.

Note: When I asked Roberta Tokumaru, 'Aikahi Elementary School's principal, for her favorite dessert, she replied, "Sponge Drops." I taste-tested it and everyone loved it! It is a little challenging when preparing it for the first time, but it gets easier.

Russian Tea Balls

Yield: 4 dozen

1 cup (2 blocks) butter, softened
4 tablespoons sifted powdered sugar
1 teaspoon vanilla
2 cups sifted flour
1 cup finely chopped nuts
Sifted powder sugar for coating

In large bowl, beat butter and sugar until light and fluffy. Add vanilla; beat well. Add sifted flour in portions and beat well each time. Mix in nuts. Chill for 30 minutes or longer for easier handling.

Form into 1-inch balls and place onto ungreased cookie sheets. Bake at 350°F for 20 minutes or until edges are golden brown. Cool on brown paper bags. Roll and dust each cookie with sifted powdered sugar.

Note: Flour should be sifted before measuring.

Almond Biscotti

1 cup sugar
½ cup butter, melted
½ teaspoon anise seed
3 tablespoons anisette or other anise flavor liqueur
1 tablespoon vanilla or brandy or whiskey
3 eggs
3 cups flour
3 teaspoons baking powder
1 cup toasted almonds (raisins or walnuts)

In large bowl, stir together sugar, butter, anise and liqueur; then beat in eggs. In another bowl, stir flour and baking powder. Add flour mix to wet mixture. Mix in almonds or fruit sprinkled with a little flour.

On a greased baking sheet, shape dough with hands to form flat loaves about ½-inch thick, 2-inches wide and as long as desired. Bake at 350°F for 30 minutes. Remove from oven and cool 5 minutes. Cut diagonally ½-inch or ¾-inch thick. Places slices closely together cut side down and bake until lightly toasted (about 10 to 15 minutes.) Check often.

Optional: Add ½ teaspoon almond extract and ½ teaspoon anise extract.

Optional: Sprinkle with powdered sugar or dip in chocolate.

Chocolate Shortbread

Yield: 8 dozen

1 pound (4 blocks) butter, softened
1½ cups sugar
1 tablespoon vanilla
5 cups flour
¾ cup cocoa powder
¼ teaspoon salt

Beat butter and sugar until light and fluffy; add vanilla. Sift together flour, cocoa powder and salt. Add in small portions to butter mixture. Use spatula to blend together. Form into balls and place on ungreased cookie sheets. Flatten and prick with fork times in 3 places. Bake at 350°F for about 20 to 25 minutes. (Do not over bake or cookies will burn.)

Note: This recipe was adapted by Jean Machida Bart based on an old Scotch Shortbread recipe from Elaine Inouye. Jean uses Herhey's dark cocoa powder but says if you want a milder flavor, use the regular cocoa powder.

Cream Cheese Brownies

Yield: 24 brownies

1 (19.8-ounce) box brownie mix (e.g. Duncan Hines®
  Dark Chocolate premium brownie mix), which re-
  quires 2 eggs, ⅓ cup vegetable oil, and ⅓ cup water

Cream Cheese Mixture:
1 (8-ounce) box cream cheese, softened
⅓ cup sugar
1 egg
½ teaspoon vanilla

Preheat oven to 350°F. Grease 9 x 13-inch pan.

Prepare brownie mix as directed on package; set aside.

In small bowl, beat cream cheese with sugar until well blended. Stir
in egg and vanilla. Spread half of brownie batter in prepared pan.
Cover with cream cheese mixture. Spread remaining brownie batter
on top. Cut through batter with butter knife several times for marble
effect. Bake for 20 to 25 minutes.

. . . .

Note: One of T.J. Goodin's favorite! T.J. was a junior at MidPac when
he shared this recipe with me. He often makes this for himself and his
family.

Lemon Bars

Yield: 24-36 bars

Crust:
1½ cups flour
½ cup powdered sugar
¾ cup (1½ blocks) cold margarine or butter

Combine flour and powdered sugar; cut in margarine until crumbly. Press onto bottom of lightly greased 9 x 13-inch pan. Bake at 350°F for 15 minutes or until golden brown.

Topping:
4 eggs, slightly beaten
1½ cups sugar
1 teaspoon baking powder
3 tablespoons flour
½ cup lemon juice

While crust is baking, combine topping ingredients and mix well. Pour over baked crust (no need to let crust cool) and return to oven. Bake 20 to 25 minutes or until golden brown. Cool. Cut into bars. Sprinkle with powdered sugar. Store in refrigerator.

Lemon Bars with Poppy Seed Crust

Yield: 16 bars

½ cup (1 block) butter, softened
¼ cup powdered sugar, plus more for dusting
1½ cup flour, divided
¼ teaspoon salt
1 tablespoon poppy seeds
2 teaspoons lemon zest
1½ cup sugar
3 eggs
½ cup freshly squeezed lemon juice

Preheat oven to 350°F.

Beat together butter and ¼ cup powdered sugar. Mix in 1 cup of the flour, salt, poppy seeds, and zest. Press evenly into 8 x 8-inch non-stick or lightly greased baking pan. Bake for about 18 to 20 minutes or until edges are golden.

While crust is baking, beat together 1½ cups sugar, eggs, and lemon juice thoroughly. Add remaining ½ cup flour and mix until well-incorporated. When crust is done, immediately pour filling over hot crust. Bake for 30 to 35 minutes or until golden and puffy.

Cool and cut into 16 squares. Dust with powdered sugar before serving.

Note: Eleanor Tokunaga emailed this recipe to me, saying, "It is excellent." I made it, shared it and got rave reviews.

Apple Bars

Yield: 24 servings

Crust:
4 cups flour
²/₃ cup sugar
1¼ cups (2½ blocks) cold butter

Filling:
4 to 5 cups apples, diced (about 4 Granny Smith
apples)
½ cup sugar
1½ teaspoons cinnamon
¼ cup flour

Mix together flour and sugar. Cut in cold butter until crumbly. Reserve 2 cups for topping, Press remaining dough into greased 9 x 13-inch pan. Set aside.

In large bowl, mix together apples, sugar and cinnamon. Add flour and mix thoroughly. Spread filling over crust. Sprinkle remaining crust mixture on top of filling. Bake at 375°F for 45 minutes or until golden brown.

....

Hint: Cut butter into small cubes before adding to flour and cutting in until crumbly.

Note: Love this apple bar dessert! It's similar to apple crisp but it's easier to take to a potluck. The apples are fresh and not from a can.

Liliko'i Bars

Yield: 24 to 30 bars

Crust:
2 cups flour
½ cup powdered sugar
⅛ teaspoon salt
1 cup (2 blocks) butter

Combine flour, powdered sugar and salt; cut in cold butter until crumbly. Press onto bottom of lightly greased 9 x 13-inch pan. Bake at 300°F for 25 to 30 minutes or until golden brown. Remove from oven and turn oven up to 350°F.

Topping:
4 eggs, beaten
1½ cups sugar
1 teaspoon baking powder
3 tablespoons flour
½ cup fresh liliko'i juice (adjust according to tartness)
¼ teaspoon lemon juice

While crust is baking, combine topping ingredients and mix well. Pour over baked crust (no need to let crust cool) and return to 350°F oven. Bake 20 to 25 minutes, or until golden brown. Cool about 25 minutes on wire rack and while still warm, loosen sides from pan and cut into bars using a wet knife. Sprinkle top with powdered sugar. Store in refrigerator.

Note: Dr. Clayton Chong got this recipe after tasting it at a restaurant in Kona on the Big Island. Thank you, Dr. Chong for sharing it. (I now grow my own liliko'i so I can have fresh liliko'i juice handy. It grows very well on a chain link fence.)

Hint: Prepare a day before and refrigerate for best results. It tastes best chilled.

Fruitcake Bars

Yield: 30 bars

Crust:
1½ cups flour
⅓ cup sugar
¾ cup butter

Mix until crumbly. Press into lightly greased 9 x 13-inch pan. Bake at 350°F for about 10 minutes or until light brown.

Topping:
½ cup sifted flour
1 teaspoon baking powder
¼ teaspoon salt
4 eggs, slightly beaten
1 cup sugar
1 teaspoon vanilla
1 cup chopped candied fruit
1 cup chopped nuts

Sift flour, baking powder, and salt together; set aside. Mix sugar with eggs and vanilla. Toss fruit and nuts in flour and add to egg mixture. Pour over baked crust and bake at 350°F for 20 to 25 minutes. Cut into bars while still warm; sprinkle with powdered sugar.

Note: At my first mochi book signing in 2000, Jean Machida Bart, my '57 Hilo High classmate, showed up with a gift of cookies to congratulate me. I was so happy and grateful to see her. I especially loved her fruitcake bars. I had to include her recipe for others to enjoy.

Date Bars

Yield: 40 pieces

1 cup (2 blocks) butter, softened
2 cups sugar
4 eggs, beaten
2 cups flour
½ teaspoon baking powder
2 cups finely chopped dates
2 cups chopped walnuts
Powdered sugar, for sprinkling

Layer 12 x 16-inch jelly roll pan with parchment paper; set aside.

Beat butter and sugar together until fluffy. Add eggs; beat. Add flour and baking powder; blend. Mix in dates and walnuts. Spread batter evenly on parchment paper. Fill in corners. Bake at 350°F for 30 minutes.

Cut while still warm. Sprinkle powdered sugar on top. Place in paper baking cups and store in plastic container.

Note: Date bars may be frozen to keep bars moist and chewy.

Teruko Matsumoto shared her delicious date bars with Ruby Saito's mother during their tai chi class at Mō'ili'ili Community Center. Ruby shared one with me. I asked for the recipe and have made it many times since then.

Energy Bars with Fruit

Yield: 96 pieces

Dried fruits:
1/3 cup raisins
1/3 cup golden raisins
1/3 cup cranberries
8 dates, chopped and floured in 1 tablespoon flour
   (use sieve to remove excess flour)
6 apricot halves, chopped
1 pear half, chopped
1 peach half, chopped
1 cup toasted sesame seeds
1¼ cups unsalted dry roasted peanuts
6 cups Quick 1 Minute Quaker® Oats
1/8 teaspoon salt
7 cups Rice Krispies®
½ cup creamy peanut butter
¼ cup (half block) butter, softened
1 pound large marshmallows

Grease 9 x 13-inch pan; set aside. In large microwaveable bowl, blend peanut butter and softened butter together thoroughly; set aside.

In large skillet, toast oatmeal on medium-low about 15 to 30 minutes, sprinkling salt over. Stir cereal every five minutes.

Heat until very warm to the palm of your hand. Add fruits, nuts, and sesame seeds. Mix thoroughly. Add Rice Krispies®; mix carefully and heat until very warm to palm of hand. Continue to keep oatmeal mixture warm on stove.

Place marshmallows on top of peanut butter mixture and microwave for 1 minute 13 seconds. (While microwaving marshmallows, place warm oatmeal mixture in very large container.) Remove bowl from microwave and work quickly to blend marshmallows and peanut butter. Add to warm oatmeal mixture and stir quickly and gently until the marshmallow mixture coats all the dry ingredients. Place mixture in pan.

With buttered fingers (or use foil or waxed paper) press mixture evenly in pan. Use another pan to help press mixture evenly. Cool. Cut into bars. Wrap in waxed paper. Need not refrigerate if consumed within one month.

Suggestion: To cut bars, first cut out a piece measuring 2 x 9-inch. Place on cutting board and cut in half, then half again, and so on until you have 16 pieces measuring 1 x 2-inch each. Do that five more times and you will have 96 pieces.

Variation: The amount of chopped dried fruits should total 1½ cups. You could omit the pear half and peach half and substitute with other dried fruit.

Note: The first time I made this it was a little difficult. Since then I've made these energy bars many times and it has gotten easier. These energy bars are the lightest and best of all that I have ever made. I have had many requests for the recipe. They are great to take along on long trips away from home.

Energy Bars

Yield: 36 bars

2½ cups Rice Krispies® cereal
1 cup Quick 1 Minute Quaker Oats®
¾ cup roasted sesame seeds
¼ cup (½ stick) butter
½ cup creamy peanut butter
1 (10-ounce) package marshmallows
¼ to ½ cup peanuts
½ cup raisins (or raisin and cranberry combination)

Grease 9 x 13-inch pan; set aside. In frying pan, combine Rice Krispies®, oats and seeds; toast for a few minutes.

In large pot, melt butter over medium-low heat. Add peanut butter and marshmallows; melt and blend over low heat. Stir in cereal mixture, peanuts and raisins. Press in greased pan with greased fingers. Cool. Cut into bars; wrap individually with wax paper or plastic wrap.

. . . .

Note: Love this! This is one of the easier energy bars to make. Gay Wong of Mutual Publishing really enjoyed this

Tsubushian Bars

Yield: 24 to 30 bars

Crust:
1½ cups flour
¼ cup sugar
¾ cup (1½ blocks) chilled butter

In large bowl, combine flour and sugar; mix together. Cut in butter until mealy. Press mixture evenly into 9 x 13-inch pan. Bake at 350°F for 15 to 20 minutes or until slightly brown.

Topping:
½ cup flour
¾ cup sugar
1 teaspoon baking powder
¼ teaspoon salt
3 eggs, beaten
1 cup chopped macadamia nuts (or walnuts)
1 (18-ounce) can tsubushian (red azuki bean paste)

While crust is baking, combine flour, sugar, baking powder and salt in medium bowl. Mix in eggs until blended. Add nuts and tsubushian; mix together. Pour mixture over baked crust and bake additional 40 to 45 minutes. Cut into bars while warm; leave in pan to cool.

. . . .

Note: At a church potluck several years ago, Henry Paolillo encouraged people to taste his wife's shortbread, saying that it's very good. I did, liked it very much and asked his wife, Vicky, for the recipe. The recipe above has a thinner crust than Vicky's original recipe since she mentioned that she prefers a thinner crust. I also reduced the amount of sugar from 1 cup to ¾ cup.

Bohemian Nut Slice

Yield: 16 pieces

1 package yeast
½ cup warm water
1 teaspoon sugar
2 eggs, separated
½ cup sugar
1 teaspoon vanilla
2 cups flour
¾ cup butter or margarine, hard and cold from refrig-
    erator, but not frozen
½ cup chopped nuts
Powdered sugar for sprinkling

Sprinkle yeast over warm water. Add 1 teaspoon sugar. Stir and let stand.

For meringue, beat egg whites until stiff. Gradually beat in ½ cup sugar. Add vanilla. Set aside.

Sift flour, cut in butter. Blend in egg yolks and yeast. Form into 2 balls. Roll out dough to 9 x 13-inch oblong size on lightly floured board. Spread with meringue and sprinkle nuts. Roll as for jelly roll. (Use a spatula to help roll.) Place on cookie sheet and make a ½-inch deep cut lengthwise down the center of each roll. Bake at 375°F for 20 to 22 minutes. Sprinkle with powdered sugar while warm.

Note: A little "challenging" to prepare, but tastes great!

ASSORTED
Treats
home made

Haupia

Yield: 16 to 24 servings

1/3 cup cornstarch
1/2 cup sugar
1/8 teaspoon salt
2 (12-ounce) cans coconut milk

Combine cornstarch, sugar and salt. Stir in 1/2 cup of the coconut milk; blend to form smooth paste. Heat remaining coconut milk and add cornstarch mixture. Cook, stirring frequently for about 20 minutes or until thickened. Pour into 8 x 8-inch pan. Cool and refrigerate. Cut into 1 1/2 inch squares.

Tapioca

Yield: 14 servings

1 cup small tapioca pearls
6 cups water
1 cup sugar
1 (12-ounce) can coconut milk

Boil water in nonstick pot. Add pearls to boiling water; stir well. Lower heat to medium and cook for 12 minutes. Stir frequently to avoid pearls sticking to bottom of pot. Cover and remove from stove; let sit for 30 minutes. Add sugar; let sit, uncovered, for 1 1/2 hours. Add coconut milk; mix well. If desired, pour into small 5.5-ounce portion cups with lids. Makes about 14 servings. Refrigerate.

Cream Cheese Kanten

Yield: 20 servings

1 (8-ounce) box cream cheese, softened
1 cup sugar (or less)
4 envelopes Knox® gelatin
¼ cup water
1¼ cups hot water
3 (11-ounce) cans mandarin oranges, drained
1 can 7-Up® or Sprite®

Lightly grease 9 x 9-inch pan.

In small bowl, dissolve gelatin with ¼ cup water. Add 1¼ cups hot water to the dissolved gelatin and stir well to blend.

In large bowl, beat cream cheese and sugar. Stir gelatin mixture slowly into cream cheese mixture; blend thoroughly. Mix in fruit and 7-Up®. Ladle liquid and fruit evenly into pan. Refrigerate to set.

Note: Shared by Betty Oishi, a retired grandmother. She often makes this for family and church gatherings. The kanten is refreshing and stays firm while being served at a potluck.

Variation: My granddaughters like mandarin oranges but their Tai Tai preferred peaches. Substitute mandarin oranges with 2 (15-ounce) cans lite sliced peaches, cut in large chunks.

Almond Float

Yield: 12 servings

3 envelopes unflavored gelatin
3 cups water, divided
1 cup evaporated milk
1 cup sugar
4 teaspoons almond extract
1 to 2 (15-ounce) cans mandarin oranges, or other
   fruits of your choice

Dissolve gelatin in 1 cup of the water. Heat evaporated milk, 2 cups water and sugar; add gelatin and stir until sugar and gelatin are dissolved. Cool and add almond extract. Pour into 9 x 13-inch pan and refrigerate to set. Cut into cubes and place in serving bowl. Pour mandarin oranges over, including syrup. (If using 2 cans of mandarin oranges, drain second can.)

Note: A very refreshing dessert! Everyone's favorite and it is one of the easiest desserts to make. For softer texture, add 3 Tablespoons more water when dissolving gelatin.

Almond Roca Bars

Yield: 72 pieces

1 box Original Hawaiian Graham Crackers® from Dia-
   mond Bakery
1 cup (2 blocks) butter
½ cup sugar
¾ cup slivered almonds, chopped

Line 2 cookie sheets with non-stick aluminum foil. Lay crackers in rows. Melt butter and sugar together until bubbly. (Remove from heat at the slightest bubble.) Spoon or use pastry brush to coat hot mixture evenly over crackers. Be sure to saturate crackers. Sprinkle nuts over crackers. Bake at 325°F for 7½ minutes then turn cookie sheet and continue baking for additional 7½ minutes until slightly brown.

Note: Do not use margarine. Baking time may vary depending on oven. Watch carefully. Do not burn bottom. You may need to adjust baking time or temperature. Jan Uesato, who emailed the recipe to me, usually buys slivered almonds from Trader Joe's and uses a food processor to chop them. She freezes the almonds and uses them as needed.

Hint: Almond Roca Bars may be frozen to be consumed later.

Cereal-Almond Brittle

Yield: 14 servings

2 cups Cheerios® cereal
2 cups Cinnamon Toast Crunch® cereal
2 cups quick oats
1 cup sliced almonds
½ cup butter
¼ cup brown sugar, packed
⅓ cup maple syrup, real or maple-flavored

Line large 17 x 14-inch cookie sheet (or two 10 x 15-inch pans) with "no stick" foil. Spray foil with cooking spray. In large bowl, mix both cereals, oats and almonds; set aside.

In saucepan, heat butter, brown sugar and syrup over medium heat, stirring frequently, until mixture boils. Pour over cereal mixture and stir until well coated. Spread mixture evenly on cookie sheet with rubber spatula until about ½-inch thick.

Bake at 300°F for 35 to 40 minutes or until almonds are golden brown. Cool completely, about 15 minutes. Break into pieces with fingers. Store in tightly covered container.

. . . .

Note: Kathryn Kato raved about this snack and wanted to share it with me. It was quite easy to make. I loved it and I couldn't stop eating it. It is so good!

Furikake Chex® Mix

Yield: about 11 quarts

3 (12-ounce) boxes Crispix®, or use Rice Chex® and
    Corn Chex® to equal 36 ounces
1 (1.3-ounce) jar aji nori furikake
1 (12-ounce) jar unsalted dry roasted peanuts
2 (8-ounce) packages (about 6 cups) premium mixed
    arare (Enjoy® brand)
1 (12-ounce) package lightly salted macadamia nuts
1 (9.25-ounce) can cashew halves with pieces

Sauce:
½ cup (1 block) butter
³/₈ cup sugar
2 tablespoons soy sauce
½ cup vegetable oil
½ cup Karo® Light Corn Syrup

In small saucepan slowly melt butter on low heat. Add sugar and soy sauce and heat until sugar is dissolved. Turn off heat and add oil and corn syrup. Set aside to cool.

Place cereal in very large aluminum pan (or divide cereal into 2 large pans). Slowly drizzle the "almost cool" sauce mixture over cereal, a little at a time, and toss to coat. Sprinkle furikake and toss gently. Add nuts and arare; toss.

Bake at 250°F for 1 hour. Mix every 15 minutes.

. . . .

Variation: Substitute other combinations of nuts and arare of your choice.

Note: Ever since my sister-in-law Amy shared this great tasting local Chex® mix with us last Christmas, it has become our favorite.

Peanut Butter Balls

Yield: 34 to 36 balls

½ cup sugar
1 cup Karo® light corn syrup
1 (18-ounce) jar peanut butter e.g. Reese's® creamy
    peanut butter
4½ cups Rice Krispies®
1 cup raisins or Craisins® (or combination of both)
1 (9-ounce) package Hershey's® Kisses candy

Before Beginning:

Scoop out peanut butter from jar into small bowl for easier handling. Unwrap 36 candy Kisses and have ready to put into center of ball. Spread a length of waxed paper in 9 x 13-inch pan for balls to cool on.

Heat sugar and Karo® syrup in large pot, first at medium low, then at medium heat, stirring constantly. Bring to boil and remove from heat. Immediately add peanut butter; stir until blended and smooth. Add Rice Krispies® and raisins and mix thoroughly. Be sure all dry ingredients are coated with peanut butter mixture. (Add more Rice Krispies®, if necessary.) Work quickly as it gets harder as it cools. Use thin disposable gloves to keep mixture from sticking to your hands.*

Scoop a heaping tablespoonful of cereal mixture, make a hole in the center and insert a Kiss, pointed end down, and cover by bringing cereal mixture over. Add more cereal mixture as needed to cover. Place balls on waxed paper. Cool before wrapping. Wrap with 6 x 8-inch pieces of waxed paper. Roll each ball in waxed paper and twist ends.

*I found Playtex® Clean Cuisine disposable gloves for handling food at Long's® and they worked very well.

Note: This snack was shared by Japan tour leader, Lionel Tashiro. It was made by his wife, Janice. Everyone enjoyed it on the long bus ride. The balls last for days without refrigeration.

Peach Crumble

Yield: 24 pieces

1½ cups (3 blocks) butter, softened
1½ cups sugar, divided use
4 cups flour
3 (15-ounce) cans lite sliced peaches, drained
2 teaspoons cinnamon

Beat butter and 1 cup of the sugar together until fluffy. Add flour and blend together. Place half of the mixture in 9 x 13-inch pan. Press down lightly.

Mix together drained peaches, cinnamon and remaining ½ cup sugar and place peaches evenly over flour mixture in pan. Sprinkle remaining half of flour mixture evenly over. Bake at 350°F for I hour until lightly browned.

Serve warm.

Note: Any leftover peach crumble may be refrigerated and warmed in a microwave.

Baklava

Yield: 24 to 36 pieces

1 (16-ounce) box phyllo sheets
1 cup (2 blocks) butter, melted
1/3 to 1/2 cup sugar
2 teaspoons cinnamon
1 cup chopped walnuts

Follow thawing directions on box. Thaw dough and unroll. Cut off I inch from layered dough lengthwise; set aside. Cut the remaining dough in half. You now have 2 sheets of layered dough to fit 9 x 13-inch pan.

Combine sugar and cinnamon; set aside.

Pour a little butter in pan to grease. Place first half of layered dough in pan. Pour about 1/3 cup of butter over dough. Tilt pan all ways so butter is spread evenly. Sprinkle sugar, cinnamon, and nuts over dough. Place the 1-inch strips of dough evenly in pan. Place second half of layered dough in pan. Cut in squares, bars, or triangles (24 to 36 pieces). Pour remaining butter evenly over dough. Bake at 325°F for 50 to 55 minutes.

While baklava is baking, prepare glaze about 20 minutes before baklava is done.

Glaze:
1/2 cup sugar
1/4 cup water
2 teaspoons lemon juice

Simmer over low heat until slightly thick (about 20 minutes). DO NOT OVERCOOK. Using a pastry brush, brush hot glaze over baked pastry soon after removing from oven. Remove pastry from pan while still warm.

. . . .

Note: Recipe from Carol Inouye. Very easy to make and not too sweet. I really like her recipe. To make triangles, cut in half lengthwise, then in thirds across. Cut each square diagonally corner to corner creating 4 triangles in each for a total of 24.

Gluten Free Banana Pancakes

Yield: 1 serving

½ ripe banana, mashed
1 egg, beaten
Oil for frying

Blend together banana and egg. Heat a little oil in pan. Drop desired amount into pan and fry both sides.

. . . .

Note: My granddaughter who is allergic to gluten found this recipe and prepared it for breakfast. It is quite tasty. Now we can all enjoy pancakes.

Chi Chi Dango

Yield: 9 x 13-inch pan

1 (16-ounce) box mochiko
2¼ cups sugar
1½ teaspoons baking powder
1½ cups water
1 (12-ounce) can coconut milk
Food color of your choice (about 4 drops)
Katakurio or kinako for dusting

Combine dry ingredients in large mixing bowl; set aside. Combine water and coconut milk. Make a "well" in center of dry ingredients, pour coconut mixture into "well" and whisk gradually from center until batter is smooth and free of lumps. Add about 4 drops of food color of your choice and blend together.

Pour into greased 9 x 13-inch pan. Cover with foil and seal tightly. Bake at 350°F for 1 hour. Remove foil carefully. Cool thoroughly for 3 to 4 hours or longer (preferably overnight). Cut with plastic knife to desired size. Dust with katakuriko or kinako.

. . . .

Note: This is my granddaughter's favorite! Why buy this mochi at stores when you can easily make a whole panful. A perfect treat for Girl's Day in Hawai'i.

Andagi

5 cups flour
2 cups sugar
7 teaspoons baking powder
¼ teaspoon salt
5 eggs, beaten
⅓ cup Wesson® oil
1½ cups water, more or less

Sift together flour, sugar, baking powder and salt in large bowl. In small bowl, beat 5 eggs and mix together with oil. Pour egg mixture into the dry ingredients. Add water, starting with less and adding enough just until completely moistened. DO NOT OVERMIX. Drop by tablespoon, using a teaspoon to scrape batter off tablespoon into hot oil (350°F to 365°F) and cook around 3 to 5 minutes, or until nice and brown. Do not crowd the andagi. They will roll around by themselves. Drain on paper towels. Test doneness by inserting a skewer through doughnut.

Hint: The next day, any leftover andagi can be placed in toaster oven at 350°F for about 15 minutes.

Note: This is the well-known Hilo andagi recipe. Easy for beginners and very tasty.

Maui-Style Baked Manju

(Yield: 60 2-inch manju)

5 cups flour
2 cups oil
¾ cup cold water
1 teaspoon salt
2 cans koshian or tsubushian

Mix flour, oil, water and salt. Form and flatten batter in palm of hand. Place scoop of koshian in center and cover with edges of dough. Pinch to seal edges. Place on ungreased cookie sheet. Bake at 350°F for 30 minutes.

Optional: Mix 1 egg yolk and 1 tablespoon cream. Brush on for golden top.

Poi Mochi

4 cups (two 10-ounce packages) mochiko
1½ cups sugar
1 bag poi
2 cups water (more or less as necessary)
Oil for deep frying

Combine mochiko, sugar and poi in mixing bowl. Add water gradually and blend well until mixture has the consistency of thick pancake batter, not watery. Drop by the teaspoonful into hot oil heated to 375°F. (Use another spoon to scrape batter off.) Fry until golden brown. Drain on paper towels.

Donna's Butter Mochi

Yield: 24 to 30 pieces

½ cup (1 block) butter
1 (16-ounce) box mochiko
2½ cups sugar
3 teaspoons baking powder
5 eggs
1¼ cups milk
1 (13.5-ounce) can coconut milk
1 teaspoon vanilla
½ cup sweetened coconut flakes for sprinkling (optional)

Melt butter. (Microwave cold butter for 38 seconds.) Set aside to cool. Grease 9 x 13-inch pan; set aside.

In large mixing bowl, combine mochiko, sugar, and baking powder; set aside. In medium bowl. whisk eggs. Add milk, coconut milk, vanilla, and melted butter; mix to blend.

Make a "well" in dry ingredients and pour in liquid ingredients. Whisk from center, gradually blending all ingredients until smooth. Pour into greased pan. Sprinkle coconut flakes, if desired. Bake at 350°F for 1 hour and 10 minutes. Cut when cool.

. . . .

Note: This is a variation of the popular butter mochi. I tasted this at a family Christmas party and really liked this version. I used our cousin Donna's name because there are so many butter mochi recipes out there with slight differences in each.

Tri-Colored Mochi

Yield: 9 x 13-inch pan

1 pound (16-ounce box) mochiko
2 cups sugar
1 teaspoon baking powder
1 (12-ounce) can coconut milk
2 cups water*
1 teaspoon vanilla
Food color, red and green
Katakuriko or kinako for dusting

In a large mixing bowl combine mochiko, sugar and baking powder. Blend water, coconut milk and vanilla. Add to dry ingredients gradually, mixing thoroughly with whisk or spoon.

Remove 2 cups of mixture. Add about 3 drops of green coloring. Pour into greased 9 x 13-inch pan. Cover with foil and bake 15 minutes at 350°F.

Pour 2 cups white mixture over first layer. Cover with foil and bake 20 minutes.

Add red coloring to remaining mixture and pour over second layer. Cover and bake for 30 minutes. Cool uncovered, preferably overnight. Cover with clean dishcloth. Cut with plastic knife when mochi is totally cooled.

Cut to desired size and dust with katakuriko.

Note: I make this for Girl's Day. Very colorful. My granddaughter loves this plain without any kinako or potato starch.

*Lessen water by ½ or ¼ cup if firmer mochi is desired. If water is lessened, measure slightly less than 2 cups for each layer.

Cocoa Mochi

Yield: 9 x 13-inch pan

2 cups (10-ounce package) mochiko
1¾ cups sugar
3 tablespoons cocoa
1 tablespoon baking soda
2 eggs
1 (12-ounce) can evaporated milk
1 (12-ounce) can coconut milk
¼ cup butter, melted
2 teaspoons vanilla

Sift together mochiko, sugar, cocoa and baking soda in a large mixing bowl. In another bowl, lightly beat eggs and add evaporated milk, coconut milk, butter and vanilla and mix. Pour into dry ingredients and mix until batter is smooth. Pour batter into greased 9 x 13-inch pan. Bake at 350°F for 1 hour 10 minutes. Cool completely.

Blueberry Mochi

Yield: about 36 pieces

1 pound (16-ounce box) mochiko
1 cup butter, melted
2 cups sugar
1 (12-ounce) can evaporated millk
4 eggs
2 teaspoons baking powder
2 teaspoons vanilla
1 can blueberry pie filling

Stir sugar in melted butter. Add milk and mix well. Add eggs and mix.
Stir in baking powder, mochiko and vanilla. Pour into ungreased 9 x
13-inch pan. Fold in the blueberry pie filling creating a marbleized
look. Bake at 350°F for 1 hour or until toothpick tests clean.

Pumpkin Mochi

Yield: 4 dozen pieces

1 pound (16-ounce box) mochiko
2½ cups sugar
1 teaspoon baking powder
1 (29-ounce) can solid pack pumpkin
5 eggs
2½ cups milk
½ cup butter, melted and cooled
2 teaspoons cinnamon
1 teaspoon ground ginger
½ teaspoon ground cloves

Combine mochiko, sugar and baking powder in large mixing bowl.
In a separate large bowl, beat eggs slightly. Add butter, milk, pumpkin
and spices; mix well. Stir into the mochiko mixture. Mix thoroughly
until smooth. Pour into greased 9 x 13-inch pan. Bake at 350°F for 1
hour. Cool for several hours before cutting.

Fresh Strawberry Mochi

Yield: 8 pieces

12 strawberries, whole or cut in halves if large
1 (18-ounce) can koshian
1½ cups mochiko
½ cup sugar
1½ cups water
Katakuriko (potato starch) for dusting

Clean strawberries, hull, and pat dry. Wrap with koshian (about a heaping teaspoonful) and set aside; refrigerate until ready to use.

Mix together mochiko, sugar, and water thoroughly until smooth. Pour into slightly oiled microwave tube pan. Cover with plastic wrap and microwave on high for 8 minutes. Sprinkle katakuriko on cutting board. Turn over mochi onto cutting board. Coat hands with katakuriko. While still hot, cut mochi with plastic knife into eight pieces. Flatten and place a strawberry covered in koshian in center of mochi. Bring edges together and pinch to close. Cover completely with mochi. Place in foil or paper baking cups.

Variation 1: Dip bottom half of strawberries in melted chocolate. Wrap mochi dough around chocolate area allowing top of strawberry to show.

Variation 2: Use tsubushian for filling. Form 12 little balls (about a heaping teaspoonful) and place on waxed paper. Refrigerate until ready to use. Cut mochi into 12 pieces for this.

Variation 3: Form little balls of crunchy or creamy peanut butter for filling in place of tsubushian. Refrigerate until ready to use.

Prune Mui

Yield: 12 cups

6 (10-ounce) packages pitted prunes
2 (6-ounce) packages dried apricots

Sauce:
1½ cups lemon juice
1 box (1 pound) brown sugar
3 tablespoons Hawaiian salt
1 tablespoon 5-spices
3 tablespoons whiskey
2 tablespoons honey, optional
1 teaspoon ground cloves (or 10 whole cloves)
1 (3-ounce) package dried lemon peel, cut into strips
　　and discard seeds
1 (4-ounce) package seedless ling hing mui, shredded

Mix together sauce ingredients in large container; add dried fruits. Mix together thoroughly. Continue to mix in the morning and at night for 4 to 6 days to marinate fruits evenly.

Note: Love this prune mui! The taste is super delicious. I combined almost identical recipes from Jane Danstuka and Joan Sato for this version. Jane uses one more ingredient which I could not find anywhere, She uses a sprinkle of see moi type red ginger. Jane makes this prune mui to give away for Christmas and I was so fortunate to be there having coffee at Ala Moana when she gave a container to me. Thank you, Jane.

Chinese Pretzels

Yield: 135 pretzels

4 eggs
1 cup milk
2¾ cups water
1¼ cups sugar
2½ cups flour
1 (16-ounce) box cornstarch
Oil for deep frying

Heat oil in electric skillet to 350°F. Heat rosette iron in hot oil. In large bowl, beat eggs with whisk. Add milk, water and sugar; mix together. Add flour gradually; blend. Add cornstarch; mix until all ingredients are blended and free of lumps (to be sure, pour batter through large sieve into another large bowl to clear all lumps.) Dip hot iron into batter, covering ¾ of the form. Return to hot oil and fry until rosette comes off iron. Turn rosette over and cook until light brown. Flip over once more and continue cooking until golden brown. Remove and drain on paper towel.

Note: Use 2 rosette irons so that one is heating up while the other is being used. The best! This recipe was developed by my sister-in-law, Amy. It has been our family's secret for over 20 years until now. Enjoy!

Apple Crisp

Yield: 24 servings

First Layer:
6 to 8 apples, pared and sliced

Place apple slices in 9 x 13-inch pan. Add more if pan is not full.

Second Layer:
½ cup sugar
½ teaspoon cinnamon
Dash of salt
2 tablespoons flour
¼ teaspoon nutmeg
¼ cup water

Mix together all ingredients and sprinkle over apples.

Topping:
1 cup flour
½ cup butter
½ cup nuts
²/₃ cup sugar
²/₃ cup oatmeal

Mix together all ingredients and spread over apple mix. Bake at 350°F for 50 to 60 minutes.

Avocado-Lime Jell-O®

Yield: 20 servings

1 (6-ounce) large box lime or lemon Jell-O®
½ cup sugar
2 cups boiling water

In medium bowl, mix together lime Jell-O®, sugar and boiling water.

Set aside to cool.

2 envelopes Knox® gelatin
½ cup water
½ cup mayonnaise
½ cup milk
¾ to 1 cup avocado, mashed

Mix together gelatin and water; set aside.

In small bowl, blend together mayonnaise, milk and avocado. Add gelatin mixture; blend. Add to Jell-O®; mix together. Pour into 9 x 9-inch pan well-rubbed with mayonnaise. Chill well.

Note: I had given Kathryn Kato some avocados from my tree and she later emailed this avocado recipe to me. Her sister had made this avocado dessert and she said it's quite good.

Tip: Avocado pulp can be frozen and it works well for this recipe. Scoop out enough avocado for 1 cup and seal in baggies for future use.

Jell-O® Kanten

Yield: 20 pieces

1 (6-ounce) box strawberry Jell-O®, or use lime or
   orange flavor
4 envelopes Knox® gelatin
½ cup sugar (or a little less)
5 cups water (½ cup tap water and 4½ cups hot water)

Pour ½ cup tap water into large bowl. Add Jell-O®, gelatin and sugar;
mix to make a paste. Pour hot water into mixture, stir to blend. Cool.
Pour into 9 x 9-inch pan slightly greased with mayonnaise. Refrigerate
to set.

Variation: Add drained diced peaches and/or lychee. Refrigerate Jell-
O® for ½ hour first before adding in fruits.

3, 2, 1 Jell-O®

Yield: 16 servings

3 cups boiling water
2 (3 ounce) boxes Jell-O®, any flavor
2 packages Knox® gelatin
1 cup heavy whipping cream

Dissolve Jell-O® and gelatin in boiling water; set aside to cool. Add
cream and mix together; pour into 8 x 8-inch pan. Refrigerate until
firm.

Note: Kids love this! They'll enjoy helping and seeing what happens
when gelatin separates into 2 layers when chilled.

Rainbow Jell-O®

Yield: 9 x 13-inch pan

6 (3-ounce) boxes of Jell-O®: 1 each of strawberry,
   orange, lemon, lime, berry blue, and grape
8 envelopes Knox® gelatin
1 can sweetened condensed milk (Eagle brand)
Hot water

Spray nonstick spray in 9 x 13-inch pan; set aside.

In small bowl, mix condensed milk with 1 cup hot water. In another bowl mix 2 envelopes gelatin with 1 cup hot water. Combine the two mixtures; set aside.

In four separate bowls, prepare the first 4 colors: strawberry, orange, lemon, and lime. Add 1 envelope gelatin to each color; mix. Add 1 cup hot water to each bowl; mix until dissolved. Add ½ cup plus 2 tablespoons of the milk mixture to each Jell-O®; mix. Let cool.

Pour strawberry mixture into pan and chill for about 20 minutes until set. (After placing the strawberry mixture in refrigerator to set, prepare the last 2 colors, blue and grape, same as the first 4.) After the strawberry Jell-O® becomes firm, carefully pour the orange mixture into pan, using a ladle. Chill for 15 minutes. Repeat procedure with remaining Jell-O® in the same order as listed.

Note: Keep pan flat in refrigerator and leave pan in refrigerator to pour in each color. Be sure each Jell-O® layer is firmly set before adding the next color or colors may merge.

A true rainbow dessert. So colorful and refreshing. Everyone loves this special Jell-O®. It was first introduced to Ruby Saito by Joyce Ito at one of their Hawai'i Yamaguchi Heritage Club meeting. Joyce often shares her delicious desserts with the other members.

Broken Glass Dessert

Yield: 24 servings

4 (3-ounce) boxes Jell-O®: 1 each of strawberry, lemon,
   lime, orange
4 cups hot water
1 quart skim milk
5 envelopes Knox® unflavored gelatin
1 cup sugar

Prepare Jell-O® a day early. Dissolve each Jell-O® separately in 1 cup hot water. Cool and refrigerate overnight.

The next day, combine skim milk, gelatin, and sugar in saucepan. Heat to dissolve sugar and gelatin. Pour into large container. Cool to room temperature. Cut Jell-O® into approximately ¾-inch cubes; fold into milk mixture. Pour into 9 x 13-inch pan. Refrigerate about 3 to 4 hours to firmly set.

Local Style Fruit Cocktail

Yield: 6 to 8 servings

3 cups jabon, peel and break flesh apart into bite-
   sized pieces
1 (20-ounce) can whole lychees, drain but reserve
   liquid
1 (15-ounce) can mandarin oranges, drain but reserve
   liquid

Combine fruits in large bowl and toss gently. Add desired amount of lychee and mandarin liquid to fruits. Serve chilled.

Note: My friend, Kathryn Kato gave me a beautiful jabon and suggested this refreshing fruit cocktail. Jabon (Japanese) is also known as bulok (Chinese) and in English as pomelo. She said that even people who don't care for jabon like this fruit cocktail.

Pistachio Fruit Dessert

Yield: 30 servings

Step 1:
2 (16-ounce) containers small curd cottage cheese
1 (20-ounce) can crushed pineapple, drained really
   well until almost no juice left
2 (8-ounce) containers Cool Whip®
1 (3.4-ounce) box instant pistachio pudding

In large container, begin with mixing cottage cheese and crushed pineapple. Mix in Cool Whip®, then the instant pistachio pudding powder. Mix together. Refrigerate 6 hours or overnight to firm.

Step 2:
2 (3-ounce) boxes lime Jell-O®
2 cups hot water

Combine lime Jell-O® with 2 cups hot water. Pour into 8 x 8-inch pan and refrigerate until firm.

Step 3:
1 (20-ounce) can pineapple chunks, drain well
2 (11-ounce) cans mandarin orange, drain well
1 (15-ounce) can sliced peaches, cut into cubes, drain well

Add fruits to chilled and firm cottage cheese mixture and mix together. Cut Jell-O® into cubes; add to cottage cheese mixture. Mix lightly so Jell-O® cubes do not break apart. Refrigerate until ready to serve.

. . . .

Variation: Add coconut flakes and mini marshmallows, if desired.

Note: This makes a lot! So plan to serve it at a large gathering. I have had so many requests for this recipe which I got from Gwen Murai who got it from Carolyn Kotomori when she served it at one of our reunion meetings.

Popo's Pickled Mangoes

Yield: 5 quarts

15 to 20 green mangoes, peeled and sliced
¼ cup Hawaiian salt

Place sliced mangoes in large container. Sprinkle Hawaiian salt over.

Let sit for 3 to 5 hours; gently tossing occasionally.

Pickle Sauce:
6 cups water
4 cups sugar
2 cups vinegar

Boil pickle sauce until sugar dissolves; set aside to cool.

Drain and place mangoes in glass jars; pour vinegar mixture over. Refrigerate.

Note: Great pickled mangoes! I received a very similar recipe from Wendy Calizar who adds 1 teaspoon Chinese five spices. Red food color is optional. Another recipe calls for 10 to 20 pieces of Li Hing Mui, if desired.

Glossary

Arare	Rice crackers
Chi chi	Milk
Dango	Dumpling
Furikake	Rice condiment
Haupia	Coconut cornstarch pudding
Jabon	Japanese name for pomelo or bulok (Chinese)
Katakuriko or **Katakuri**	Potato starch
Kanten	Agar agar, made of seaweed that jells at room temperature*
Kinako	Ground roasted soybean flour
Koshian	Smooth bean paste
Liliko'i	Passion fruit
Ling Hing Mui	Preserved and seasoned Chinese plums (also, li hing mui)
Mochi	Glutinous rice or sweet rice flour
Mochi Crunch	Arare, rice crackers
Mochiko	Glutinous rice flour
Prune Mui	Prunes seasoned with Chinese spices
Tsubushian	Coarsely ground red bean paste

* The use of the word "kanten" in this cookbook refers to the consistency of the Jell-O® dessert that can remain firm at room temperature by using Knox® gelatin.

Index

About the Author

Jean Watanabe Hee has been gathering and testing recipes since she retired from teaching in 1999 which led to her Hawai'i's Best cookbooks. Prior to that, she taught at the elementary level in several Windward schools and loved it. Her last school was 'Aikahi Elementary where she taught kindergarten. Some of her former students still keep in touch with her.

After retiring, besides her time spent in gardening and traveling, she found that she enjoyed cooking and baking. This led to creating her cookbooks of favorite recipes for everyone to enjoy.

She still lives in Kāne'ohe with her husband, Don. In 2015, they lost their second daughter, Jennifer, to a brain tumor. She had been married to Tony Metcalfe for only four years, and she is dearly missed by family and friends. Her older sister, Cheryl, still lives on Maui with her husband, Earl. Their older daughter, Rachel, graduated from Puget Sound in 2016 and their younger daughter, Kristen, attends North Carolina State. Our daughter and two granddaughters are a big help and comfort to us. They also enjoy cooking and have shared some of their recipes with me.